The World

of the

Talmud

The World

of the

Talmud

by Morris Adler

SECOND EDITION

A Hillel Book
SCHOCKEN BOOKS · NEW YORK

This volume is one of a series of "Hillel Little Books." Developed by the B'nai B'rith Hillel Foundations, the books in this series deal with issues of fundamental importance to Jewish college students. Written by men of variant points of view, they are intended to stimulate further study and discussion.

First SCHOCKEN PAPERBACK edition 1963

Seventh Printing, 1976

This edition is published by arrangement with B'nai B'rith Hillel Foundations, Inc.

Library of Congress Catalog Card No. 63-18390

Manufactured in the United States of America

CONTENTS

The World

of the

Talmud

I

BY WAY OF PREFACE

The Talmud represents a remarkable achievement, incorporating within itself a rich cultural mosaic which no one who is interested in significant historic, intellectual and social patterns can afford to ignore. Despite the fact that the Talmud speaks in an idiom peculiarly its own and is framed in a context of a specific culture, it is stamped, as all great accomplishments of the human spirit are, with universal significance and relevance. The Talmud thus represents one of the monuments in the culture of mankind.

The Talmud is the creation of a people through its gifted representatives. These spokesmen were rooted deeply in the history and tradition of their group. They were not men of affairs in the conventional sense of the term, though they were far from being withdrawn from the common life; nor were they political leaders or empire builders, legislators or administrators, scientists or philosophers, economic barons or artists. They conformed to none of the hero-patterns upon whom the Western world has usually conferred leadership. They were teachers, — that was how they regarded themselves, though in the process of serving as teachers of people they also performed functions that were judicial, administrative and political in character. The subject of their instruction was an ethico-religio-cultural tradition. Hence they were concerned with the preservation and transmission of a body of teaching that centered its interest upon the meaning of life, the dignity of man, the determination of right and wrong, ethical relationships between men, the social good and the inner life of the individual. These are obviously not parochial problems. These are the issues with which every age is recurringly confronted. Here the most recent word is not necessarily the wisest word. Subsequent researches and studies in this area of thought and human behavior do not automatically invalidate earlier reflection as they often do in the case of natural science and technology. A modern man who rejects unstudied the ethical doctrines of the past on the ground that their chronological priority renders them hopelessly antiquated, is a prig and worse. He denies himself and the contemporary society of which he is part the insights which not alone deserve a hearing, but which may well be in advance of any his own generation may, by its unaided efforts, attain. Modern man who has not shown any remarkable talents in the ordering of his life in terms of high ethical standards, should not cut himself off from any of the significant resources in this domain. The Talmud is a great repository of wisdom and sensitivity and is concerned with the ever urgent need of translating its recognitions into active forces in man's individual and social life. What is here suggested is not necessarily a return to the Talmud and its prescriptions. We have a more modest and limited objective. Those who deal with this sphere of human experience and aspiration would do well not to omit a consideration of this Rabbinic literature. Its synthesis of the legal and ethical, the moral and social, the universal and particular, may be exceedingly rich in suggestion and inspiration, even for a culture and an age as far removed as are our own from those of the Talmud.

For many American Jews, acquaintance with the main outlines of Talmudic content and method might be an adventure in self-definition and self-identification. They live with a vague awareness of their Jewishness. A vague sentiment links them to it and a decent respect for ancestry and self prevents them from denying their Jewish inheritance, amorphous though it may appear to them. We can identify ourselves only in the social context in which we move. When that social context is cloudy, our understanding of self must likewise suffer from ambiguity or uncertainty. American Jews cannot appreciate or understand their grandfather or great-grandfather, to go no further back in their ancestry, when they are entirely unfamiliar with the influence which Talmudic lore and law exerted upon the earlier generations. Nor can they develop a sound attitude to the traditions and practices which they encounter in their own experience without a measure of awareness of the place the Talmud occupied in shaping them. A philosophy of modern Jewish living, worthy the attention of intelligent Jews, cannot be constructed unless it pay attention to the Talmud as one of the great moulders of Jewish doctrine and outlook.

An additional factor provides further justification for yet another attempt to explain the world of the Talmud. Probably no other work in world literature has been as consistently maligned and as fiercely condemned as has the Talmud. It is a work that is paradoxically little known and greatly misjudged. It has been censored, banned and publicly burned. The history of its persecution, it has been said, parallels that suffered by the people that created it. A determined and continuing attempt at "bibliocide" has been made against it. It was charged not only with defaming the Christian faith and its founder, but also with fostering depravities and perversities in those who adhered to it. Doctrines and laws were imputed to it as infamous as any that the human imagination at its most diabolic could devise. Indeed the Devil was said to be its author. The most recent vicious attack upon the Talmud was made by Alfred Rosenberg, the so-called philosopher of the Nazis, in a book called *Immorality in the Talmud*.

A distinguished group of Christian scholars have studied the Talmud and refuted the vile allegations about it. They have treated it as an important phase of historic Judaism and interpreted its true character. The most patent absurdities are no longer repeated except perhaps by some ranting bigot whose very extremism discredits him in the eyes of reasonable people. Yet on another level a harmful misconception of the Judaism whose authoritative exposition is embodied in the Talmud still persists and is widely accepted by otherwise well-intentioned people. I refer to the evil associations which in the lore and literature of Western civilization still cling to the words Pharisaism, Pharisaic Judaism and Pharisee. Rabbinic literature is the masterwork of Pharisaism and modern Judaism pervasively bears the stamp of Pharisaic influence. The identification of Pharisaism with formal legalism, smugness, self-righteousness, hypocrisy, rigorous observance in the total absence of any inwardness, goes back to the New Testament. One encounters this view in essays, newspaper-editorials, sermons and addresses and even in the columns of journals that pride themselves on their liberalism. Terms like Pharisaic complacency and hypocrisy are used to stigmatize political and ideological opponents. Several years ago Stalin designated deviationists from official Communist policy in Russia as "Talmudists." In this sphere there seems to be no "Iron Curtain" between the East and the West. The work of scholarship in exposing the unfairness of the above characterization of the Pharisees has not yet dispelled this persisting error.

Jews who are integrally linked to Western civilization can easily become heirs to and victims of this deeply-rooted, centuries-old false evaluation of their own background. In so doing they give strength to a perversion of the truth, though in innocence, and muddy their own self-respect as Jews. Even a modest knowledge of the nature of the Talmud, its development and purpose, should aid in dispelling this miasma of falsehood and enable Jews to see their past and themselves in a truer light.

II

ATTEMPTING A
DEFINITION

Any attempt to describe the Talmud, its nature, development and method is beset with difficulties. There is the practical impossibility of defining the term in quick order. An oversimplified description may well amount to a distortion. Many centuries ago, a heathen asked a great sage for a definition of Torah, brief enough not to extend beyond the time the questioner could balance himself "on one foot." The achievement of the sage has remained unique since his time. And even at that, the teacher concluded his concise statement with the admonition "go, study."

The Talmud is a large and diverse work. It is the product of a millennium of intellectual, spiritual and cultural activity. Many generations participated in its formation. Its sprawling text covers innumerable subjects. A literature of vast proportions has grown up about the Talmud. Each of its sixty-three tractates and many of their individual sections and passages have given rise to prolific commentary. At this very moment in a Yeshiva in America or Israel a learned rabbi is discoursing on some portion of its text. Young students are even now bent for many long hours over its pages, some nourishing the hope that they too may bring to it the offering of a commentary of their own, with original interpretations and analyses. It is impossible to compress the scope and character of the universe of discourse, amplification and inquiry which is the Talmud into a single definition. Its methodology and the organization of its material present another obstacle to easy understanding. Perhaps we can approach the subject best by indirection following the counsel of Solomon Schechter who, in an essay on "The Study of the Talmud,"[1] pointed out that it is easier to indicate what the Talmud is not than to affirm what it is.

The Talmud is *not* a code though it contains cases, laws and legal decisions. It is *not* a history though it abounds in historical information and is so indispensable a source-book for the period it covers that those who have written of that era without adequate knowledge of the Talmud have been invariably betrayed into error. It is *not* a biographical dictionary though innumerable sages and scholars are cited in it and in many instances valuable information about them is provided. It is *not* an anthropological treatise, yet is a mine of folklore. It is *not* a theological tract though Rabbinic thought is a major element in the Jewish outlook. It does *not* present us with a philosophical system, yet perceptive students have found an organic unity underlying its rich diversity. Encyclopedic in scope, it is not an encyclopedia nor is it designed as such. It is a book neither of religion nor of history nor of ethics nor of philosophy, yet each of these disciplines and others are embraced by it. Indeed the Talmud is not a book at all. It may more appropriately be described as a literature.

Yet even this designation is neither precise nor particularly illuminating. The term "literature" suggests a series of books authored by individual writers, each devoted to a specific genre, poetry, drama, essay, belles-lettres, philosophy, religion or science. The Talmud on the other hand comprises sixty-three tractates or volumes, none of which is the work of a single author. Nor is any volume rigidly limited to the treatment of a single subject. All of the types of material found in the entire Talmud may often be represented in a single volume.

The Talmud, to suggest a positive description, is the extensive record of the intellectual, social, national and religious activity pursued by Jews during the approximately thousand-year period of its formation. It is a university in literary form, mirroring the culture of its group. The Talmud, however, is more than an anthology of reflections and conclusions. It embodies within itself the process as well as the achievement. It reveals the actual working of the minds of individuals and of schools of thought as they grappled both with the issues of their time and with those larger questions of meaning and destiny which are the perennial concern of the human mind and spirit. It includes the itinerary followed by their thought as well as the destination at which it arrived. Not being a book that came from a single hand, nor a series of volumes representing the planned accomplishment of a scholarly body, the Talmud is organic in its growth and reveals to the open-eyed student the varied layers of its own evolution.

The Talmud, then, to employ the term we have used in the absence of a more precise one, is a literature. It lacks that consciousness of effort which possesses the literary craftsman, or that artistic drive which impels the creative spirit to express his private vision. Nor is it the work of ecstatics lost in mystic communion. It is the work of men who dwelt in the midst of society and were intent upon fashioning a godly community. In seeking to translate into reality the tradition they inherited, they expanded, renewed and deepened it so that it could continue to function with unweakened relevance in the midst of changing circumstances. Though the tradition had its origins in divine revelation, its study and application were given over to men. In that task, man was not called upon to renounce his God-given faculty of reason, nor to surrender his initiative and judgment. For within the broad places of Israel's inheritance there was ample room for the exercise of logic, deduction and human decision. To interpret the words of the Torah did not mean self-restriction to a limited and specialized area of interest, but the enlargement that comes from dealing with moral purposes and ethical values. Beyond the detail and transcending the rite was the greater task of bringing into the daily life of a people the abiding accents of a divine law that pervades the universe and thus to enrich the passing scene with intimations of eternity. The tradition, as the Rabbis viewed it, was the bridge between a noble past and a great fulfillment. In guiding men across it, they were investing human life with depth and purpose.

III

THE RISE OF THE
ORAL LAW

We have spoken of the tradition to the preservation and elaboration of which the Rabbis devoted themselves. At the center of Judaism is the tradition or, if you will, a Book; in Christianity, it is the figure of a man. A Christian scholar suggested this significant difference when he wrote, "Pharisaism is a religion of ideals, Christianity of an ideal person." If we substitute for the word "Pharisaism" the more inclusive term "Judaism," it stands as an essentially true description of a basic contrast. Judaism has its heroes and immortals. However, no figure, not even the towering one of its Lawgiver Moses, is enshrined and hallowed in any form calculated to make him comparable to the central figure in the Christian faith. Jewish teachers could contemplate, as their Christian counterparts could not, that the validity of their tradition did not depend on even their greatest mortal. The Rabbis say that Ezra was worthy of receiving the Torah from God at Sinai, had not Moses preceded him. Others too merited the mantle that rests upon Moses. The personality of no individual is so inextricably bound up with the tradition that his absence from it would affect its validity.

This fundamental diversity between the two faiths helps explain the different paths each faith followed in its development. The centrality of the Book in Judaism gave rise to the formation of the vast litera- ture which grew up about the Bible and of which the Talmud is the most important example.

On the return from the Babylonian exile in the middle of the fifth century B. C. E., Ezra and his associates consciously elevated the Torah to primacy in the economy of the Jewish life they hopefully desired to re-establish. They did not stumble upon such an emphasis accidentally. It was implicit in the nature of the tradition almost from the outset. It is to Ezra's enduring credit that he recognized this in-dwelling characteristic of his people's faith and that he set about with determination to make the Book the foundation of the community's life and the chart of individual behavior. "For Ezra had set his heart to seek the law of the Lord, and to do it, and to teach in Israel statutes and ordinances" (Ezra 7.10). In this verse from Ezra, the Hebrew word here translated "to seek" is "lidrosh" which may also be rendered "to interpret." It sug- gests the method by which the Torah was to be made a functioning force relevant and applicable in the midst of the changes to which men are subject. The Torah was to be enlarged by interpretation, and the Hebrew word for this process is derived from the root of the word Ezra employed. The process is "Midrash" — interpretation.

A group of teachers arose to teach and interpret the Law. We shall see later that the term Law is a wholly inadequate and indeed erroneous translation of the word Torah. We use the term because it has won widespread acceptance and is therefore convenient even when we do so with reservations. This new class of Interpreters and Expounders was known as *Soferim*, generally translated as Scribes. The term "Scribes" has become a judgment word and is heavily freighted with negative evaluations. In the New Testament it appears by the side of the word "hypocrites," and reiteration for many centuries has made them all but synonyms in many minds. Hebrew scholars, however, point out that a more correct rendition of the title "Soferim" by which these teachers became known is "Bookmen" or "Men of the Book," rather than Scribes.

A great convocation was held and Ezra brought out the Torah before the assembled multitude and he read its words before them. The Biblical account of this occasion declares, "and they read in the book, in the law of God, distinctly; and they gave the sense and caused them to understand the reading" (Nehemiah 8.8).

The first task of the Men of the Book was to make its words known. They sought to teach its contents to the people. They wished to have it serve as the text-book of the community. But their aspirations went far beyond that. The Book might have been accepted as a classic: its words entering popular speech; its poetry embellishing the rhetoric of speaker and writer, and nothing more. Their purpose, however, was to make of the Book the primary guide to action and belief; its words and teachings the motivation of good attitudes and habit, the inspiration to good life and noble character. They strove for nothing less than that the book function as the vital and effective central authority in communal and personal life.

In a sense, their aim was revolutionary and precipitated a struggle that was to last for several centuries. If the Book was to be the greatest source of authority, the power of the Temple and its priesthood would inevitably contract. The center of influence would shift from the priestly class that inherited religious position and privilege, to teachers and expounders drawn from all strata of society. Religious knowledge would no longer remain the esoteric possession of a caste — as it was in all ancient religions — but become quite literally an open book for the entire community. The period of the Soferim heralded a democratic religious and cultural revolution in the life of the Jewish people.

When the Men of the Book attempted to translate their intention into reality, they were confronted by difficulties. The Book was regarded as divine in origin and character. It was the record of a historic revelation of God's will and law. Philo was to describe this view centuries later in these words, "The provisions of this law alone, stable, unmoved, unshaken, as it were stamped with the seal of nature itself, remains in fixity from the day they were written until now, and we expect them to abide through all time as immortal, so long as the sun and moon and the whole heaven and the world exist."[1] The Book represented for the Men of the Book no transitory legal system born of the passing conditions of one era, limited in its scope, confined in its authority, standing in constant need of revision and correction. This was not man-made jurisprudence, partial and incomplete, written in terms of the prevailing needs and circumstances, out-dated by changing circumstances. This was a final book, all-embracing, adequate for every contingency. No future, however distant and revolutionary, could possibly render it antiquated. The words of a later sage pithily expressed what was in their mind, "Leaf it (the Book) and leaf it yet again, for everything is in it."[2]

This was the conception that governed the Men of the Book, and the premise upon which their approach to the Book was predicated. However, in seeking to effect the transition from the word to the act, the Soferim soon found themselves confronted by palpable difficulties. The content of the Book did not always lend itself to ready implementation. Divine in origin and character, it was nonetheless obscure in some places. Its words did not always yield clear directions as to conduct. There were passages of uncertain intent and words whose connotation was not known. Frequently a law or institution was cited in so general a way that the lack of detailed prescription did not indicate the procedure to be followed in its observ-ance. Some laws were rehearsed several times in the Bible and the reason for the repetition was unexplained in the text. Nor was the Book entirely free from apparent contradictions.

In a divine book, these obscurities and difficulties could not be attributed to lapses by the Author. They could be explained only as resulting from insufficient study and inadequate comprehension on the part of its mortal readers. Even as nature, fashioned by the same hand that wrote the Book, does not reveal at first glance the laws by which it functions, the Book does not yield its full meaning at first reading. The intent, hidden beneath surface discrepancies and perplexities, will be brought to light through exploration, patient study, diligent and dedicated probing. Its implementation depended upon the determination of its meaning through proper interpretation. This method, to which allusion has already been made, was called Midrash — the seeking out, through interpretation, of the actual intent of Biblical doctrine and statute. Indeed the Men of the Book did not feel that they were originating this method of exploration. Since the Torah was a law of life whose words were meant to be translated into belief and action, many supplementary, oral interpretations were said to have been transmitted to Moses simultaneously with the written text. From the outset, the Book was fringed by supplement and commentary. The Torah could be understood and practiced only in terms of its accompanying oral elaboration. Imbedded in Torah were all the instructions necessary for compliance with its laws and for the full comprehension of its doctrines and narrations. The Men of the Book and their successors did not believe that they were adding to the text but that they were educing from and reading *out* of the Bible the meanings which from the very beginning had been enclosed within it. At no time were they reading *into* the text what was not meant to be there. There were signs all through the Torah by which its intention could be established. There were rules of interpretation which, if followed, would help students elicit from the text its true purport wherever the words themselves were unclear. Theirs was a work of discovery, not of innovation. They saw themselves where the Torah was concerned, as interpreters, not legislators.

The Men of the Book had a good reason for their belief that the Written Law of Moses was supplemented by oral explanation from the outset. Already in their time observances and customs were in vogue among Jews for which the Torah, literally understood, offered no warrant. There also was a popular lore which was obviously an extension of the narratives of the Bible. Only through oral interpretation could the Torah become operative in every phase of the life of the community. To develop the interpretation adequate to this purpose was the function of the Men of the Book.

Some of the specific difficulties which the written text of the Torah presents will illustrate the nature and purpose of the work of the Men of the Book.

If there is any belief which Judaism has always stressed and upheld it has been its uncompromising affirmation of One God. Yet the Torah, in telling of the creation of the first man, puts these words in the mouth of God, "Let us make man in our image, after our likeness" (Genesis 1.26). What is the reason for the plural in this context?

In one of the paragraphs which became part of Judaism's central prayer, the Shema, we are commanded "And thou shalt bind them for a sign upon thy hand, and they shall be for frontlets between thine eyes. And thou shalt write them upon the doorposts of thy house and upon thy gates" (Deuteronomy 7.9). The word for "frontlets" in the text is "letotofot," whose precise and etymological meaning was no better known then than it is now. How does one implement the words of such a section? What is the nature of the object we are to place on the doorpost, how is it to be made, of what material and what is it to contain? Assumed by and implied in such a presentation is supplementary description.

All through the Bible the institution of marriage is taken for granted. Less than fifty verses after the Bible opens God declares "It is not good that man should be alone; I will make a help meet for him." Six verses later we are told, "Therefore shall a man leave his father and his mother, and shall cleave unto his wife and they shall be one flesh" (Genesis 2.18, 24). The patriarchs take wives unto themselves. The kin who are prohibited from marrying each other are clearly enumerated. Yet nowhere in Scripture is the procedure of solemnizing a marriage described. A verse in Deuteronomy states, "When a man taketh a wife and marrieth her, then it cometh to pass, if she find no favor in his eyes, because he hath found some unseemly thing in her, that he writeth her a bill of divorcement and giveth it in her hand and sendeth her out of his house" (Deuteronomy 24.1).

Men who wished to follow this law could not do so if they relied exclusively on the explicit words of the Torah. What is "an unseemly thing"? Rabbis were later to differ widely in their interpretation of the Hebrew phrase so translated. There were those who believed that it meant "adultery" and that the Scriptural law therefore laid down the principle that divorce could be granted only when the woman dishonored her marriage vow. Others took a more lenient position and permitted the dissolution of marriage on many other grounds. The text as it stands does not explicitly state its meaning. It seems to invite interpretation. Nor is the verse more helpful in the matter of the drawing up of the "writ of divorcement." The Bible speaks of "Sefer Kerithut," literally a "book of rending asunder." The phrase seems to suggest that a definite form was in vogue. We do not know from Biblical law what its nature was. The husband is given the right to draw up such a writ. Does he have recourse to any legal or religious authority? What if the husband be illiterate or incompetent to prepare this document? Is there a constituted body that issues the divorcement and confers validity upon it? The text itself does not resolve these dilemmas and questions.

The Bible admonishes "Thou shalt not take vengeance or bear a grudge" (Leviticus 19.18). Do we have a redundancy here, a mere verbal flourish? This, however, is unthinkable in a divinely inspired text. What then is the meaning of the apparent reiteration of the same idea? Does the repetition veil ethical

27

instruction not apparent on a superficial reading of these words?

The inevitability of a commentary or an extension of the written text is probably best illustrated by the laws governing the Sabbath. In unmistakable language the Israelites are enjoined from labor on the Sabbath. Its sanctity is related to the very creation of the world, "And God blessed the seventh day, and hallowed it; because that in it He rested from all His work which God in creating had made" (Genesis 2.3). In the Ten Commandments, the seventh day is explicitly ordained as a day of rest. Indeed, Scripture ordains capital punishment for a violation of the prohibition to work on the Sabbath, "Six days shall work be done, but on the seventh day there shall be to you a holy day, a sabbath of solemn rest to the Lord; whosoever doeth any work therein shall be put to death" (Exodus 35.2). Yet there is no enumeration of the forbidden types of labor. What constitutes work is a question crucial to the institution of the Sabbath, yet no answer is provided. The kindling of fire is prohibited (Exodus 35.3). Work was forbidden even during the season of plowing and harvesting (Exodus 34.21). The cryptic injunction "let no man go out of his place on the seventh day" (Exodus 16.29) is another specific instance of the general principle establishing the Sabbath as a day of rest. These few particular definitions of labor on the Sabbath were not meant to exhaust the list of forbidden work. The admonition to refrain from work is so strongly worded and the reference to it so recurring and emphatic that it becomes clear that the Sabbath was meant to be marked by a more complete cessation of work than the few and meagre specific designations would indicate. Somewhere in the Scripture there must be a guide to its intent with regard to Sabbath rest. Indeed even before the days of the Men of the Book other types of work were traditionally classified as forbidden, despite the absence of clear instruction in the Torah. The prophet Isaiah admonishes the people that doing business on the Sabbath or indeed even talking about it constitutes a desecration (Isaiah 58.13). Jeremiah censures those who bear burdens on the day of rest (Jeremiah 17.21). Amos indicates that trading on the Sabbath is not permitted (Amos 8.5). As Moore points out "These are plainly only casual instances of a much more comprehensive customary law, which was probably extended in the course of time to meet changing conditions."[3] The Written Law, it was believed, was meant to be understood in the context of an oral commentary which accompanied it.

Sometimes a conflict of laws is encountered in the Torah without any suggestion of how it is to be resolved. Thus the circumcision of a male child is to take place on the eighth day after his birth. If the eighth day coincides with the Sabbath, which of the two institutions ordained in the Torah, circumcision and Sabbath rest, is to give way?

We have by no means exhausted the types of problems which had to be met if the Bible was to function as the basic authority in the life of the community and command the respect and loyalty of the people. Particular laws, if understood in the form they were expressed in Scripture, offended the developing moral sensibilities of the people. "Eye for an eye" was not a law that could be taken literally. Most scholars doubt that it ever was so understood. An acceptable interpretation was needed that would not weaken the authority of the Bible and yet permit greater latitude in interpreting its words. New situations demanded new interpretations. The law of the cancellation of debts in the Sabbatical year, the seventh year known as Shemitta, offered difficulties when trade and commerce assumed greater importance. The old law worked hardship upon those who desired to observe it. No situation however new could be out of the range of a revealed law, nor could a provision of a divine code be abrogated. This is where oral supplementation and interpretation stepped in.

The shapers of the Oral Law found authorization for their activity of interpretation and elucidation in the Sacred Writ itself. The reasoning of the Rabbis is illustrated by the following example. The Bible declares "If there arise a matter too hard for thee in judgment, between blood and blood, between plea and plea and between stroke and stroke, even matters of controversy within thy gates; then shalt thou arise, and get thee up unto the place which the Lord thy God shall choose. And thou shalt come unto the priests and Levites, and unto the judge that shall be in those days; and thou shalt inquire; and they shall declare unto thee the sentence of judgment" (Deuteronomy 17.8, 9). The rabbis pointedly comment on the phrase, "that shall be in those days." They ask, "Could we have possibly thought that one would go to a judge other than in one's own day?" The meaning is that one should have recourse to the judges of one's own time and accept their judgment, and thus fulfill the verse in Ecclesiastes which declares "Say not how was it that the former days were better than these?" On the same page of the Talmud they declare that the humblest and most ungifted judge is to be regarded in his age as Moses or Aaron or Samuel were in theirs.[4]

This process was not a deliberately planned one, nor was it as consciously pursued as our description might suggest. The Men of the Book and those who followed them, felt that in studying and re-examining the Book they would find in the text itself the answers to their needs. The divine Book, they believed, was and always will remain, the source of instruction and guidance in all circumstances to the end of time.

IV

WHY ORAL?

Though scholars are still debating when the "Oral" Law was first recorded in writing, it seems certain that for many years it remained an unwritten supplement to the Bible. These oral "addenda" included traditions, discussions, legal opinions, historical data and interpretations of doctrine and practice.

A modern student would be puzzled by the entire phenomenon of an expanding legal system which is exclusively entrusted to the memory of its teachers and students. The fallibility of human memory and the enormity of the material make the entire procedure seem utterly unreasonable. There are some indications that specific collections of oral law were written down. However, they seem to have been kept in the private possession of individual teachers and were not circulated publicly. In his introduction to his great code, Maimonides states that from the time of Moses to that of Rabbi Judah Ha-Nasi, the Oral Law was not taught in any academy out of a written text. The head of the academy may have noted down for himself the traditions he received from the masters under whom he had studied. In the academy, however, no teacher ever used any written material. Indeed even when the Mishna appeared in written form it continued to be called "Oral Law." For many centuries there existed a determined opposition to the writing of Oral Law. One sage, Rabbi Johanan ben Nappaha, as late as the third century C. E., firmly supported an interdict on writing and went so far as to say that "he who writes down the oral laws is as one who burns the Torah." Another scholar states categorically that those things that were meant to be taught orally may not be committed to writing. What are the reasons behind this strange refusal to record, in writing, something that was regarded as important and authoritative?

A number of considerations gave rise to the feeling that the Oral Law was to be transmitted solely by way of mouth. The Jew had one written Torah and one alone. The writing of the Oral Law might mistakenly be regarded as giving it equal status with the Bible. Another written text might cast a shadow upon the unique and supreme authority of the Torah.

The process of writing a large text in Rabbinic times was both a difficult and costly process. Few could own copies, even of Scriptures. Rabbi Meir once came to a Jewish community in Asia Minor and could not find a single copy of the Scroll of Esther. Being a scribe by profession and a scholar by avocation, he was able to write one from memory. Permission to write the Oral Law would not have changed the situation in those times in any considerable way. Only a handful of individuals could be expected to possess a copy.

The Rabbis saw themselves primarily as teachers. They may have felt that the writing of the Oral Law would have inevitably meant its condensation into a mere code, an outline of decisions and practices. The discussions, the steps taken to arrive at conclusions, the reasoning and the clash of views, would of necessity have been eliminated. The dry recital of laws could never serve as an adequate text of instruction. A law that was written down would also tend to become invested with finality and therefore discourage further development. The written text is static alongside the living word. As teachers the Rabbis were interested in preserving a vital and direct interaction between teacher and pupil. A text sometimes becomes a paper curtain intervening between the two, serving to disrupt direct communication. Exposition, elaboration, stimulation are replaced by reliance on a text. Dependence on memory gains precedence over intellectual activity. Several centuries after the completion of the Talmud a great scholar writes, "For when a pupil sits before his master who is engaged with him in studying Jewish law, the teacher recognizes the student's inclination, knows what is understood by him and what is not; what is clear and what is not, and so he can explain the subject until it is grasped and mastered. How can this be done when the law is in writing since there is a limit to what can be written."[1]

Perhaps a realization of this truth is to be found in an idiom current in the English language. We speak of "reducing" something to writing. The transition from the spoken to the written word, especially in the field of education, may represent a diminution and a weakening of the intensity and effectiveness of communication. The Rabbis say with regard to prayer, "Prayer should not be recited as if man were reading from a document." One sage advised that we should not permit our prayer to descend to routine. Another advised that a new prayer be uttered every day. The application of these observations to education may not be far-fetched.

The Talmud scoffs at those who are "laden with books," people who have acquired much knowledge but little comprehension; who know the conclusions but not the principles which underlie them or the process of thought which led to them. In the great academies of Eastern Europe the stress was on *kennen lernen*, understanding the method of study, comprehending the logic and discipline of deduction and reasoning rather than upon the volume of material one succeeds in storing in one's memory. Total recall is not yet scholarship and a good memory does not of itself insure that one is educated.

Jewish thought sensed a pedagogic danger in reliance upon a written text and felt that the best means of communication between teacher and student is by way of mouth. The vitality and drama of the interaction between master and student were preserved in a tradition that remained largely oral.

V

THE MISHNA

The Oral Law continued to grow rapidly. Each generation multiplied accretions to the expanding body of law, lore and doctrine. At the end of the second century C. E., Rabbi Judah Ha-Nasi (the Patriarch) assembled and edited a compilation of Oral Law, known as *Mishna*, meaning "study." It gained immediate acceptance as the authoritative work in the field of interpreting and amplifying the contents of Scripture including as well Rabbinic enactments, which particular circumstances required and which did not enjoy the ultimate authority of laws derived from interpretations of the Bible. Nowhere in the work is

Rabbi Judah Ha-Nasi specified as its redactor and compiler. He is, however, universally regarded as the scholar responsible for gathering into a single text the material he believed worthy of preservation. The Mishna has retained a position of authority second only to the Bible itself.

An early account states that Rabbi Judah was born on the very day that Rabbi Akiba met a martyr's death (135 C. E.), justifying the comforting belief held by a people subject to recurring attack and oppression that the sun sets in one place only to rise immediately in another. Rabbi (as the editor Rabbi Judah Ha-Nasi is always called in the Mishna, in tribute to his prominence) was a descendant of Hillel. He studied under one of the distinguished teachers of his day, Rabbi Judah ben Ilai. He was a man of aristocratic bearing and spirit as well as of great affluence. He is reputed to have been on intimate terms with the Emperor Antoninus.

Rabbi's compilation was the most comprehensive of its time and displaced all other similar collections. The heads of academies probably taught their students out of compilations they themselves had gathered and edited. We know, for instance, that Rabbi Akiba assembled the material available to him into a Mishna. The vast accumulation of material made Rabbi's compilation necessary. The diversity of Mishnaic collections emanating from the various schools required the redaction of a text which would include the basic material and replace the variety of conflicting digests of Oral Law. From the numerous miscellaneous collections, many of them unrecorded save in the memory of devoted scholars, Rabbi selected, sifted and gathered the product of centuries of discussion and deliberation. He abbreviated, summarized and rejected as his scholarship and editorial wisdom guided him, and organized the laws and discussions into a systematic work.

Rabbi and his associates were also moved to undertake the gigantic labor of compiling the Mishna by their desire to furnish a text which to some degree would function as a code by providing a norm for decisions by the sages midst the wide-ranging diversity of opinions and legal views contained in the several collections of oral law in vogue in the academies. Rabbi Simeon ben Yohai pointed out that a divine promise assures us that the Torah will not be forgotten in Israel, as it is written "for it shall not be forgotten out of the mouths of their children" (Deuteronomy 31.21). The sage seeks to reconcile this verse with another which declares "they shall run to and fro to seek the word of the Lord and shall not find it" (Amos 8.12). The latter verse means that they will not find a definite decision or a clear Mishna anywhere. Rabbi Simeon is pointing out the danger that will arise when, because of the multiplicity of opinions, there will be no one clear and definite ruling.

The Mishna, however, is not a code cataloguing laws and practices in dry and precise manner. For it was meant to be more than a guide for the rendering of accepted and authoritative decisions. It was meant, in the words of George Foot Moore, to be "an instrument for the study of Law, an apparatus of instruction." Hence it embodies not alone decisions but also legal principles, not alone the view of the majority which was to be followed by subsequent sages but also the minority opinion which from a strictly practical view had only academic value. Professor Ginzberg points out that of 523 chapters contained in the Mishna only six are free from disagreement between the authorities. The text thus provides a basis for study, for an examination of premises and conclusions, and for a comparative study of the differing views which it included. The students were to be stimulated to follow the process of reasoning used by the masters whose views are recorded in the Mishna. It was not desired to make the Mishna a stop-gap to independent thought and analysis but a stimulant to logical deduction, inference and analysis. In summary we may say that the reasons which prompted the gigantic work which Rabbi undertook in the compilation of the Mishna were fourfold. First, the enormous growth of oral law scattered over so many diverse collections called for a single authoritative text. Second, the desire to provide some measure of uniformity in the interpretation of the law dictated the editing of the Mishna. Third, there was a necessity to provide an organized text to become the basis of instruction in the academies of higher Jewish learning. Finally, there was an apprehension that a recurrence of political disturbance or oppression might endanger the survival of the Oral Law, unless it was preserved in a single authoritative collection. A gap of one generation caused by social upheaval would prove fatal to the preservation and transmission of an oral law unless it were assembled and recorded.

The Mishna, as it was organized by Rabbi Judah Ha-Nasi, was the product not of one man or one age. Its contents are not to be regarded by any means as new and original. The Mishna is the culmination of the thought and teaching of the preceding generations during which the Oral Law grew and developed. Canon Danby, in the Introduction to his translation of the Mishna, thus explains its nature, "The Mishna may be defined as a deposit of four centuries of Jewish religious and cultural activity in Palestine, beginning at some uncertain date (possibly during the earlier half of the second century B. C. E.) and ending with the close of the second century C. E. The object of this activity was the preservation, cultivation and application to life of 'the Torah' in the form which many generations of like-minded Jewish religious leaders had learned to understand this law."

Let us take a closer look at this work which might be said both to have ended one era and to have inaugurated a new age.

The word "Mishna" stems from a Hebrew root meaning "to learn" as a derivative of the primary meaning "to repeat," "to rehearse." Learning is achieved by a tireless process of reiteration, reexamination and recapitulation. When the term Mishna is used without any qualification, it refers to the work edited by Rabbi Judah Ha-Nasi. It may also mean a single paragraph or section of that work, in contrast to "Mikra" which refers to a single verse in Scripture.

The designation Mishna may likewise be applied to any of the collections of earlier teachers. Thus we may speak of the Mishna of Rabbi Akiba or the Mishna of Rabbi Meir. It means the content of the teaching contained in these collections as well as the method followed. For there is an important difference between the approach of the Mishna and that associated with the other type of Rabbinic literature known as Midrash. The latter attaches its elaborations and comments to a verse of Scripture. The verse is always cited and serves as the starting point for the extended meanings which the Oral Law wove about the specific Scriptural statements. Examples drawn from a homiletical Midrash and from a legal or halachic Midrash may help clarify the method employed by Midrash.

A verse from the Song of Songs is cited, "I am love-sick" (or "sick from love"). Then follows the comment, "The Congregation of Israel says to God, 'Lord of the world, all the sicknesses which Thou bringest upon me are only for the purpose of making me love Thee ... All the sicknesses which the nations bring upon me are only because I love Thee.' "[1]

"All are equal before the Law. The duty of its observance is incumbent upon all. For the Law is 'the inheritance of the Congregation of Jacob' " (Deuteronomy 33.4). "It does not say 'Priests' or 'Levites' or 'Israelites,' but 'the Congregation of Jacob.' "[2]

"The wages of a hired man shall not abide with thee till the morning" (Leviticus 19.13). "This applies also to the hire of animals, or of utensils or of fields. So too does a man violate the law if he withholds a hired man's wages even if the employee did not come to him to ask for the wages. The Bible says 'with thee' (namely, the responsibility rests upon 'thee', viz., the employer). A wage earner hired for the day must be given pay for the following night; one engaged for the night, for the following day."

"In righteousness shall thou judge thy neighbor" (Leviticus 19.15). "You must not let one litigant speak as much as he wants and then say to the other, 'curtail your argument.' You must not let one stand and the other sit."

The Midrash thus serves as a vast running commentary upon Scripture and it attaches itself to the Biblical verse whose meaning it elaborates. The Mishna, however, becomes, so to speak, physically independent of the text of the Bible, though in spirit and content it remains, to be sure, bound to and based upon the Torah. A verse of the Bible may be cited as proof, but a Rabbinic law becomes a "Halacha" with an identity of its own, distinct from the verse. We have interpretation of the subject in the spirit of the Torah and with full acceptance of the supreme authority of the Torah, but not necessarily associated with a specific Scriptural verse or passage. The Mishna is not a running commentary. It is a distinct structure of law and lore, rising upon the foundation of Torah but operating within the orbit of its own rules of interpretation, inference and deduction. While subordinate to Scripture in authority, it is a complementary legal code, with a measure of autonomy in its own right.

The following examples taken from the Mishna may prove helpful in seeing how the Mishna method diverges from that of the Midrash.

If a man was half bondman and half freedman (having been jointly owned by two partners, only one of whom set him free), he should labor one day for his master and one day for himself. This was the view of the School of Hillel. The School of Shammai said to them, "You have arranged it well for his master, but not for him, the slave seeing that he cannot marry a bondwoman since he is half freedman, on the one hand, nor a freedwoman on the other seeing that he is half bondman. May he then never marry? Was not the world created for fruition and increase as it is written 'He created it not a waste, but formed it to be inhabited' (Isaiah 45.18). In the interest of human welfare the remaining master is compelled to set him free and the bondman writes him a note of indebtedness for half his value. The School of Hillel changed their view and taught in conformity with the view of the School of Shammai.[3]

Even as the law prohibits fraud in buying and selling, it forbids fraud that is committed through the spoken word. A man may not say [to a merchant] "How much does this article cost?" if he does not intend under any circumstances to purchase it [the fraud involved is the raising of the merchant's hopes]. If a man who had sinned has repented, one may not say to him "remember thy former deeds." If a man was descended from proselytes it is forbidden to say to him "remember the deeds of thy fathers," for it is written, "And a stranger thou shalt not wrong, nor shalt thou oppress him" (Exodus 22.20).[4]

The separation of the Oral Law from a necessary and direct dependence upon the actual text of Scripture permitted its development as a separate and distinct entity. We have seen that the earliest teachers of the Oral Law were known as Soferim, Men of the Book. The sages of the Mishna are called Tannaim (singular, Tanna), "repeaters," "students and teachers." The language of the Mishna is Hebrew, though linguistic elements from Aramaic, Greek and Latin found their way into Mishnaic Hebrew and thus testify to a significant interaction between the Jewish and other cultures. The style of the Mishna is compact and precise, shunning rhetorical extravagance and ornamentation. There is an evident striving for clarity and conciseness. The Mishna escapes dryness and rarely deteriorates into unredeemed severity and legal dullness. For one thing, the drama of controversy is present almost throughout the Mishna. The clash of differing opinions and opposing interpretations enlivens even passages dealing with abstruse and technical subjects. For another, the Mishna does not hesitate to venture frequently on excursions into the more attractive fields of narrative, biographical account or reminiscences, homiletical exposition and ethical and doctrinal discussion. The following examples illustrate the tendency of the Mishna to punctuate its text with controversy and incident.

If a man hired laborers and bade them to work early or work late, he has no right to compel them to do so in such places where the prevailing custom is not to work early or not to work late; where the local practice is for the employer to provide them with sweetstuff he must do so. In a word, everything should conform to the custom of the place. It once happened that Rabbi Johanan ben Matthias said to his son, "Go and hire laborers for us." He went and undertook to feed them. When he came to his father, his father said to him, "My son, even if thou settest before them a banquet like King Solomon's in his time, thou wilt not have fulfilled thy duty towards them (for they spring from a noble lineage) since they are the sons of Abraham, Isaac and Jacob. But rather before they begin work go and say to them, 'On condition that I am not obliged to give you more than bread and pulse only.'" Rabbi Simeon ben Gamaliel says, "It was not necessary to speak thus, for everything follows local usage."[5]

The Mishna is divided into six main divisions called Orders. In Hebrew these divisions are termed Shisha Sedarim, Six Orders. (The Talmud is, therefore, often called "Shass," a word composed of the first letter of the words Shisha Sedarim. In many synagogues of Eastern Europe there was, as there still is in some synagogues in America, a Chevra Shass, comprising a group of men who daily studied the text of the Talmud.) It was Rabbi Akiba who developed this arrangement in order to systematize the enormous material of the Oral Law. Each order includes a number of Massechtiyot or tractates or volumes. This Hebrew term is derived from a root meaning a weaving and corresponds to the origin of our word "text" from the stem likewise signifying weaving, as in textile. There are in all 63 tractates. Each tractate is divided into chapters. Each chapter, called a "Perek," is further subdivided into sections called, in the Babylonian Talmud, a "Mishna." (In the Palestinian Talmud, which we shall discuss later, each section is called a "Halacha.") A brief enumeration of the contents of each of the six orders of the Mishna suggests the wide scope of its subject matter.

I — Zeraim (Seeds). The eleven tractates in this division deal with laws of benedictions and prayers, laws pertaining to agriculture and fruits of the field, the Sabbatical year, tithes and offerings to the priests.

II — Mo'ed (Festivals). This division embraces twelve tractates devoted to the laws of Sabbath (the tractate "Shabbat" is the largest in the Mishna), the High Holy Days, Passover and the Paschal sacrifice, the Temple tax, the festival of Succoth, Fast Days, Purim, the work that may be done and that which is prohibited, the methods of observance, etc.

III — Nashim (Women). In the seven tractates of this order we have discussions centering on marriage, betrothal, divorce, levirate marriage, vows, the trial of the wife suspected of unfaithfulness, etc.

IV — Nezikin (Damages). This order of ten tractates deals with the phases of law that we would include under the terms civil and criminal law. We have here the laws of damages and compensation, property, trade, employer-employee relationships, real estate, inheritance, court procedures, testimony, evidence, punishment for criminal offenses, the administration of oaths, and regulations associated with the idols and pagan practices of neighboring peoples. Nezikin includes also the best known of the tractates of the Talmud, that of Abot, the Ethics of the Fathers. This famous volume, frequently incorporated in its entirety in the Prayer-book, demonstrates the continuity of the Oral Law with the Law of Moses and cites ethical maxims by many of the teachers of the Mishna.

V — Kodashim (Sacred Things). The eleven tractates in this division largely treat of the laws related to the Temple and its sacrificial cult. Animal sacrifice, meal offerings, proper method of slaughtering the animals, the first-born of man and animal, pledges and the profanation of sacred things, Temple furnishings and practices are the chief subjects dealt with in Kodashim.

VI — Tohorot (Purifications). We have in the twelve tractates of this order a treatment of vessels that are rendered ritually impure, such impurity being caused by contact with or proximity to a dead body. The order deals with the uncleanness of leprosy, methods of purification, the menstrual impurity of women, and with the impurity of those who are afflicted with unclean issue from their body.

Explicit Scriptural ordinances were not the only source for the vast legislation that is to be found in the Mishna. Practices long in vogue, oral traditions, inferences and deductions from Biblical verses and regulations derived by a unique system of intepretation, all became part of the Oral Law and all were regarded as invested with unquestioned authority.

The point has been made before that the Mishna was not intended to be a one-purpose work. Meant to be a text for the students in the academies, it was also to serve as a guide for the teachers who were called upon to render decision in controversy and inform the people as to correct practice. Unmistakable signs are found in the Mishna, despite the fact that it unfailingly records both sides where there is a difference of view, as to which view is preferred and to be regarded as authoritative. Opinions that are offered anonymously, without mentioning the name of the teacher who held them, are to be accepted as the norm of practice or principle to be followed. Where an opinion is attributed to one sage, but the opposing view is introduced by the phrase "but the sages say," or "in the view of the sages," the latter interpretation is the one to be adhered to in practice.

The Mishna thus served an immediate purpose in establishing a basis for greater uniformity in practice. Yet there is much material in the Mishna that was already academic at the time Rabbi issued it. The loss of political independence and the destruction of the Temple rendered inoperative that large part of the Mishna which deals with Temple ritual and sacrifices. It did not occur to the sages to eliminate such material from a work that addressed itself, among other aims, to a most practical goal. The ultimate basis of the Oral Law was Scripture and its enactments and regulations are informed, it was believed, by a timelessness which their divine origin conferred upon them. The eternal cannot be upset or dissolved by the upheavals and the configuration of events and circumstances that take place on the more limited stage of human affairs. To eliminate these laws would be to refute the very theory from which the interpretations of the Rabbis derived their authority. But the reason that prompted the inclusion of such laws was not merely doctrinal. The Rabbis did not regard these laws as purely academic and unrelated to life. Rooted in their world-view was a firm belief in the restoration of the Temple, the sacrificial cult and political independence. The laws of sacrifice and of criminal law were as carefully and devotedly studied as the laws of Sabbath observance, dietary disciplines and the recitation of prayers. So compelling was the hope that all through the centuries in academies everywhere, in North Africa, Spain, Eastern Europe, students regarded the laws of sacrifices, criminal procedure, purifications, priestly ritual, as belonging properly to the category of relevant and indispensable knowledge which the faithful Jew should master.

Kindred to the Mishna edited by Rabbi Judah Ha-Nasi is a work known as Tosefta. The term means "Supplement" and it includes sections of earlier collections of Oral Law as well as material that did not find its way into the authoritative work of Rabbi Judah. Subsequent additions, originating after the death of the editor of the Mishna, are likewise included in the Tosefta. Like the Mishna, the Tosefta is divided into tractates, though the organization of the subjects varies from that of the primary work. Isolated passages that became disassociated from the collection of which they were part, or somehow survived collections which had been lost and were not ingathered by the Mishna are known as Baraitot, meaning "external to" or "outside of." They are sometimes cited by later authorities in the discussions which developed about the Mishna. Thus, while Rabbi Judah Ha-Nasi's text did not embrace all the available material, it is the supreme work of the Oral Law, exerting an incalculable influence on its subsequent development.

VI

THE GEMARA

We have seen that a significant portion of the Mishna was no longer applicable to existing conditions by the time its compilation had been completed. Yet the problem in law is not with its patently obsolete parts but with its apparently operative sections. Law, in a sense, freezes life at the instant of legislation. But life goes on. New situations arise which are not provided for in the code if its literal meaning alone is invoked. New conditions and experiences bring about a change of view to which the earlier promulgation does not do justice. Hence Judaism, once again, as in the case of the Mishna, had recourse to its proven and classic method of interpretation. But now it was the Mishna, not the Bible which became the subject of interpretation and elaboration.

The Mishna was complementary to the Bible. Now an extension of the Mishna was developed. It is called the "Gemara," from an Aramaic root meaning "study" or "instruction." The Gemara is sometimes also called Talmud, although the term Talmud is more generally applied to the entire Oral Law embracing both Mishna and Gemara. The Mishna is several times more voluminous than the Scripture on which it is based. The Gemara which represents the extension of the meaning and application of the Mishna is in turn many times larger than the text from which it takes its departure.

Before we examine the Gemara more closely, it will be helpful to recapitulate the concept of Oral Law which underlies it. The Rabbis did not conceive of the Written and the Oral Law as two disparate and independent systems. They were basically one, the Oral Law being the source for the authentic under-standing of the intent and the provisions of Scripture. The interpretations of the Oral Law are imbedded and implied in the Written. Maimonides, in the intro-duction to his "Mishneh Torah" states, "All the Sinaitic ordinances were transmitted to Moses with their interpretations." The Oral Law was believed to have been included in the original covenant. A Biblical verse (Exodus 34.27) declares, "Write thou these words, for after the tenor of these words I have made a covenant with thee and with Israel." The phrase "the tenor of these words" alludes to the spoken interpretations which accompanied the Written Law. One of the sages, with this verse as his authority, does not hesitate to conclude that "The Holy One Blessed be He established His covenant with Israel for the sake of the Oral Law alone."[1] Indeed it may be said that "the words that were transmitted orally are the more valuable" (Hagiga, chapter I). The Rabbis did not feel that they were introducing anything extraneous into the text. Their activity was designed to elicit from it the meanings that were implicit, though not always explicit in it. There were general statements or concepts in the Torah that had to be analyzed and translated into detailed instruction before they could be implemented. One of the eminent jurists of our time, Judge Learned Hand, pointed out an exact parallel when he discussed the perennial responsibility of the law to define "broad clauses on which the conduct of a free society must in the end depend," which the Constitution itself does not pause to define. He cites such examples as "freedom of the press," "establishment of religion and the free exercise thereof," "unreasonable searches," "due process of law," and "equal protection of the law" — as requiring constant interpretation and redefinition. The code must be explored anew in the light of a generation's new needs.

The Rabbis were governed, as we have already pointed out, by yet another consideration. As men of affairs and judges, they found themselves confronted by new situations with which the basic law had not dealt. As men of faith they were convinced that the

Torah was divine in origin and that, therefore, there could not arise a circumstance which it had not anticipated. The only way to reconcile that apparent conflict was to follow the counsel of one of their colleagues, "Search in it (the Torah) and search in it yet again, for everything is included in it." Out of this intensive "search" in the Torah, the Mishna had emerged; out of this intensive "search" in the Mishna, the Gemara emerged. To be sure, the Mishna was not divine in the same direct and literal sense as was the Torah. But it might be said of it that it was divine at a remove, since it was the authentic and, in a figurative sense, the foreordained interpretation of a divine text.

The Mishna is concise and not given to lengthy discursive argumentation, though it does record the controversies between various schools and between individual teachers. The Mishna, however, is definitely intent upon brevity. The Gemara, on the other hand, may be described as a full-scale transcript of the give and take of the discussions in the academies. It is alive with debate and the clash of differing opinions. It bristles with challenge and argument. It is prolix and allusive. It reflects the freedom and latitude which oral discussion encourages. It does not hesitate to digress and wander afield when a term, a law, an incident or reference to a particular teacher lights up an association with or stimulates the recollection of something not related to the main line of the argument. The citation of a verse suggests another and not necessarily relevant interpretation or comment. As in all good conversation, much of the charm and interest derive from the admixture of the incidental, anecdotal and even fanciful with the solid core of a consistent and informed exposition of a view. A large part of the Gemara is non-legal in character. The broadest definition of the term "law" could not possibly include the range and variety of material found in the Gemara. A wise teacher would interrupt a lengthy and difficult legal argument with a digression of a less taxing and more edifying nature. The sages declare that one should not disdain the parable, though unimportant in itself, since it can be a valuable aid in acquiring understanding of the words of the Torah. They characteristically offer a parable in defense of the parable. They say that it may be likened to a king who has lost a precious pearl and finds it by the light of a candle costing a trifle. Thus we find legend and history, contemporary science and folklore, Biblical exegesis and biography, homily and theology woven together into what, to one unfamiliar with the ways of the academies, would seem to be a curious medley of unorganized data drawn from a baffling number of unrelated categories. The Gemara does, however, return to the original subject though the digression may spread over several pages. What the argument, by reason of this apparent looseness of method, may seem to lose in directness and cogency, the Talmud gains in breadth and vitality. To pursue the Talmudic treatment of a specific subject, you cannot turn to an index, look up the particular volume in which the subject is discussed and relax in the assurance that you have exhausted your study. The same subject is dealt with in many places and in several of the sixty-three volumes of the Talmud. One particular tractate may contain the locus classicus of the particular law or decision. Yet for thoroughness one would have to examine the other volumes where, though this subject may be introduced only casually or as an excursus in an argument in another theme, the treatment may have serious import for the analysis of the concept and cannot be ignored.

The free and wide-ranging manner of the Talmud does not detract from the legal and intellectual acumen and profundity of its treatment and analysis. It remains to this day one of the most incisive and penetrating legal systems ever to be formulated. Its apparent discursiveness and its hospitality to the extraneous and incidental enable it to mirror the life of the centuries during which it grew, in an infinitely more comprehensive way than it could have possibly done if it had hewn strictly to a rigid line of legal discussion and interpretation. It is the life of its times and not only the law that we find in its pages. It is thus not simply a fundamental text for the study of the development of Jewish law, nor only an indispensable source of material for the historian nor exclusively an invaluable guide in tracing the evolution of Jewish religious concepts and practices. It is all these and more. It is a profoundly significant human document revealing the variety of universal aspirations, needs and responses of men as suggested by this literature created by a specific society during approximately a half-millennium. The Talmud presents us with no still-life portrait, but with a stream of life, active, restless. vital within its banks.

Two versions of the Gemara exist — the Palestinian, also known as the Jerusalem Talmud, and the Babylonian Talmud. Since many of the sages of Babylonia studied in Palestinian academies and since there were close relations between the two communities, it is not unusual to find the same teachers cited in both versions. Both Talmuds are, of course, based on the same Mishna and differ only in the Gemara. Of the two, the Babylonian is the larger and more fuller in its treatment. It is generally regarded as the more authoritative and has been more widely studied in the academies to this day.

According to Professor Louis Ginzberg, one of the world's great Talmudic authorities who has made an intensive study of the Palestinian Talmud, the version developed in Palestine was primarily intended for teachers and judges rather than for students in the academies. It is, therefore, more concise. Its Aggadic or non-legal sections are likewise more limited than those of its Babylonian counterpart.

The outbreaks, fierce and recurring between Jews and Rome in the middle of the 4th century finally led to the destruction of the famous seats of learning in the homeland. The academies at Tiberias, Sepphoris and Lydda crumbled. As in the days of the Hadrianic persecutions more than two centuries earlier, many fled from Palestine to Babylonia. The Palestinian Talmud was compiled towards the end of the fourth century. It is the product of the several schools that had flourished in Palestine, though its redaction took place in Tiberias. Unlike the Babylonian version which freely incorporated the folklore and popular demonology of its time, the latter under the influence of Zoroastrianism, the Palestinian Talmud excluded fanciful tales about angels and demons. Despite its greater brevity, it is more repetitious than the better-edited Babylonian Talmud and abounds in more inner contradictions. The Diaspora selected the Babylonian Talmud as the preferred version and it became universally recognized by all Israel while the Palestinian was generally neglected both in the Near East and in the great academies in Eastern Europe closer to our own time.

The Jews in Babylonia formed a great and creative community in the valley of the Tigris and Euphrates — the territory that is today included in modern Iraq. A distinguished academy arose in Nehardea which was destroyed in 260 C. E. It was removed to Pumbeditha and together with the academy at Sura guided the intellectual and religious life of Babylonian Jewry for several centuries. The most noted of the early teachers were Rab and Samuel, students of Rabbi Judah Ha-Nasi. Rab had studied in Palestine and had returned to Babylonia in 219 C. E., invested with renown as an important scholar. He served for a while as the Commissioner of markets, supervising correct weights and measures, being appointed by the Resh Galutha or Exilarch, who was at the head of the government-recognized autonomous community of Babylonian Jewry. Rab founded the academy at Sura which became the greatest center of Jewish learning in the land. His work is eloquently epitomized by the Talmud in the statement that Rab found an open and abandoned field and hedged it about. It is said that 1200 students crowded the lecture halls at Sura. His colleague Samuel, who, in addition to his great Jewish learning, was also a distinguished astronomer, headed the school at Nehardea. Two months of the year, Adar, the month preceding Passover, and Elul, the month before the High Holy Days, were set aside for assemblies for study to which farmers, artisans and tradespeople were invited. Such was the reverence for learning and the eagerness for knowledge that prevailed in the community, that we are told many thousands came at these occasions. These times were designated "Hodshei Kalla," which probably means "Months of Assembly." Dr. Schechter, taking advantage of the coincidence that "kalla" also means bride in Hebrew, termed these great gatherings "spiritual honeymoons."

The two academies of Pumbeditha and Sura were the most notable academies, although lesser schools also existed. Here students engaged in intensive study. The interpretations and discussions served to clarify and amplify the text of the Mishna and keep it viable as the basis of legal and religious decisions and enactments. The fifth century witnessed an outbreak of restrictive measures and legislation directed against Jews. The kings, determined to make Zoroastrianism not alone the state religion but also the religion of all of the inhabitants of the empire, pursued a vigorous policy of repression. There took place enforced conversions of Jewish children, the burning of synagogues and the prohibition of fundamental Jewish observances. Many Jews sought refuge in other lands. The darkening clouds dictated the wisdom of collecting, organizing and editing the vast material which had been accumulating through several centuries of study and discussion. The pioneer in this herculean task, the scope of which only the most scholarly could estimate, was Rabbi Ashi, who headed the academy of Sura for more than a half century (375–427 C. E.). His recognized many-branched learning, his spotless character and saintly life and the prestige he enjoyed superbly qualified him for this massive responsibility. He devoted more than fifty years to the work of assembling and collecting the material. His successors continued the task he had so devotedly undertaken. The final work of editorial selection and revision was done by Rabina, who died in 500 C. E. With Rabina, the Talmudic period comes to a close.

The Gemara found in both the Palestinian and Babylonian versions does not constitute a commentary on the complete Mishna. Whole sections are missing. The first edition of the Palestinian Talmud which was published in Venice in 1523 concludes with the words "Thus far we have found what is contained in this Talmud and we have made futile attempts to obtain the missing portions." Of the six orders embodied in the Mishna, we find no Gemara at all for the fifth (Kodashim, "Holy Things" devoted to the sacrificial cult and other matters pertaining to Temple service) and only for three chapters of a single tractate of the sixth, Tohorot (dealing with ritual purity).

Several chapters of tractates in other orders are also missing. In the Babylonian Talmud there are likewise gaps and in the first and sixth orders the Gemara is limited to only one tractate of the Mishna in each. The arrangement in the two versions differ. In the Palestinian Talmud the entire Mishnaic text on which the Gemara in that chapter is based, appears at the beginning, divided into paragraphs, each paragraph being called a "Halacha." In the Babylonian version, on the other hand, each paragraph of the Mishna is immediately followed by the portion of the Gemara which constitutes the commentary to it. Each paragraph is called a Mishna.

The first edition of the Mishna appeared in Naples in 1492 and was the work of the Soncino Press. The first complete edition of the Talmud was published by a Christian, Daniel Bomberg, in Venice between 1520–1523.

Unique among all the classical books that have been published is the pagination, the system of the numbering of the pages. The numbering of the pages of the Talmud established by the first edition has been followed by all subsequent editions. Hence, when a Talmudic citation is given, the page alone is noted without any reference to the edition. Whether a particular edition was published in Hamburg, Vilna or New York, the pages are numbered in precisely the same way. If one should examine, for example, page 72a of the tractate Sanhedrin in any of the editions during the more than four centuries of the printing of such editions, it will be found that in every instance

the page begins and ends with exactly the same word.
I do not know the same fact to obtain in the case of
any other classical work which has undergone repeated
publications for several centuries in several different
lands. One of the most famous and most widely used
editions of the Talmud was issued in Vilna. The
twenty large and well-printed volumes contain, in
addition to the text of the Mishna and Gemara, many
medieval and modern commentaries. It is a monument
to the Jewish community in Eastern Europe where it
appeared and which was so brutally and so completely
destroyed by Nazi savagery.

VII

HALACHA AND AGGADA
LAW AND LORE

Two mighty currents are discernible in the large
and open sea of Oral Law, namely, Halacha and
Aggada, the former referring to law, prescribing action, binding and authoritative, the latter the non-legal
element, created by the free imagination both of
individual teachers and folk fancy.

"Halacha" is the accepted Hebrew term for law.
This connotation of the word is not found in the Bible,
but first occurs in the Mishna. It stems from the root
meaning "to walk, to go," and its derivative signifi-

cance is therefore a "way of life." Seldom is a single word as richly seeded with the suggestion of an outlook, a point of view, indeed a theology as is "Halacha." We do not know the sage who first employed the term in this connotation, but he belongs to the select class of mankind's geniuses who have enriched the history which hid their very name from us.

The supremely significant place which Halacha occupies in the economy of Judaism has helped give currency to the charge that it is a faith dominated by legalism and a legalistic spirit. That this spurious allegation is repeated by a variety of sources and has endured for centuries proves once again that an error is often both contagious and sturdy. The truth of the Rabbinic statement that the sage has, ever since prophecy ceased in Israel, inherited the mantle of the prophet is attested to by more objective and more recent students. The prophets' passion for righteousness, their abhorrence of injustice, their universal outlook, their vision of a day "when the earth will be filled with the knowledge of the Lord as the waters cover the sea" and "nation shall not lift up sword against nation" inform and elevate Rabbinic legislation. R. Travers Herford, who has devoted many years of a long life to the study of Rabbinic Judaism, concludes that "nothing is farther from the truth than to say that Pharisaism made the Jewish religion, the religion of the prophets, into a hard and barren formation with no spiritual value in it. The truth rather is that the Pharisees took up the religion of the prophets and brought it to bear upon the lives of the people in a way and to an extent which the prophets had never been able to accomplish. And paradoxical though it may sound, it is not far from the truth to say that if it had not been for the Pharisees and what they did, the prophets would never have been heard of. Be this as it may, the Pharisees certainly developed their ideas of the unwritten Torah and the Halacha based on it with a clear and conscious reference to the teaching of the prophets." Legalism implies that the law becomes its own end and that the mass of legal technicality and procedure obscures the end to which the law is properly a means. The legalist does in the realm of law what the fanatic, according to Santayana, does in the sphere of life, namely, redouble his effort as he forgets his aim. In every legal system great attention is of necessity paid to methodology, to precedent, to correct procedure. For the law seeks to bring order into man's life guiding and liberating it by rule and code. Proper procedure is in a society of law the best safeguard of the rights of men. Law at its best has its eyes upon a purpose beyond itself, namely, the improvement of the lot and the advancement of the welfare of the people for whom it legislates.

The great goals of which Jewish law was conscious were both social and spiritual. The self-same men to whom the opprobrium "legalist" has been attached by the uninformed or the scornful (both qualities being frequently combined in the same critic) not only drew up laws, but composed prayers and disseminated lofty ethical teachings. Dr. Solomon Schechter points out that it was the Rabbinic tradition which assigned for public reading on Yom Kippur the fifty-eighth chapter of Isaiah, as well as the legal selection from the Pentateuch. This union of one of the most spiritual passages of the Bible with a reading containing legal enactments dramatizes the emphasis the Rabbis placed upon purpose and inwardness. We have pointed out that the Rabbis did not function as theologians. They developed no systematic creed, no definitive and explicit summation of belief. Yet no group of men were more God-conscious and more devout. Their chief interest was in having their people act in accordance with the will of God. The act was not a substitute for an inner feeling, it was an expression of it. "Theologizing" was alien to them.

The challenge by which they felt confronted, was to weave into the pattern of daily living and habitual relationships a constant sense of duty to God and His divine will. The presence of God was to be felt not alone in the Sanctuary, but also in the mart, in the home "when thou goest by the way, when thou liest down and when thou risest up." The great aim was not to make men slaves of the law, but to free them, in the midst of their mundane preoccupations in a world that eloquently speaks to their senses and appetites, for devotion to a higher life and a higher way. It was more than an inspired word-play that identified the word *harut*, laws engraved on the tablets, with *herut*, freedom. This was a cardinal principle with the Rabbis, that the law can be man's most effective instrument for freedom. Though in a far different setting and growing out of another conception and background, the decision of the founding fathers of America to insure liberty by making this "a government of laws" and not of men, bears a definite kinship with the Rabbinic view.

What worship does sporadically on festive occasions the Rabbis sought to achieve as a constant influence. Service of God was for them not only the utterance of the lips in moments of exaltation, but the faith by which we normally live, expressed through act, effort, deed. Religion is not a matter of living on the "peaks" of experience. That is for the saint and the mystic. More fundamentally, religion must mean transposing to a higher level of spiritual awareness and ethical sensitivity the entire plateau of daily living by the generality of men. Idolatry is defeated not by recognition of its intellectual absurdity alone, but by a life that expresses itself in service to God. Selfishness and greed are overcome not by professions of a larger view but by disciplines that direct our energies, our wills and our actions outward and upward. Study and learning are not to be left to the happenstance of leisure or to the occasional upsurge of interest or curiosity, but are to be made part of the daily regimen of religious activity.

The law was therefore no meaningless and dull burden for the Jew since it was both opportunity and privilege. The traditional Jew through the ages would not have comprehended such judgments as "the curse of the Law," "the dead weight of the Law," "the letter that killeth the spirit." He spoke of "simha shel mitzvah," the joy of personal fulfillment that comes from observing the Law. God in His love of Israel multiplied commandments. The Law not only linked the Jew to God, but likewise integrated him in a community. It filled his life with festive occasions and exalted moments and provided him with a redeeming and blessed instrument by which to rise above the routine and prosiness of daily existence. To this day the morning worship service includes the words, "Happy are we! how goodly is our portion, how pleasant our lot and how beautiful our heritage."

The aims of the prophets guided the rabbis in their work. One of the greatest students of Rabbinic Judaism decries the "misunderstanding (which) has arisen regarding the nature of the transition from the Prophets to the Scribes, from biblical Judaism to rabbinical Judaism." He goes on to say, "The intellectual endeavors of the Scribes are apt to be considered as a degeneration and decline from the idealism which pervades the conception of life laid down in Scriptures. The truth is that the Scribes succeeded where the Prophets had failed. Through them the teachings proclaimed in the schools of the Prophets became the common property of the whole people."[1]

The Halacha rests upon the basic premise that Judaism is a revealed religion and that God is Lawgiver as well as Creator. God's will is embodied in the Torah, from which can be educed all knowledge and laws required to govern human life. Halacha is the bridge between man and the godly life. Law in Judaism never became a discipline independent of religion and ethics. It is in the last analysis the instrument of religion and ethics. A modern scholar expresses this idea in the following words, "A peculiar character is given to rabbinical laws, however, by the fact that the interpretation of the civil and criminal legislation with its elaboration and amplification in the unwritten law is not purely juristic but is consciously guided and controlled by the moral and social principles which are equally a part of the divinely revealed Torah. In technical phrase, Jewish ethics are impressed upon the Halacha, as well as expressed in the Haggada."[2] Halacha is simultaneously the law of a community and of its religion. Such a law, in a more consistent way than secular law, is concerned with motive as well as action, with unenforceable attitude as well as with behavior that can be regulated. The test is not only "is it legal?" but also "is it right?"; the concern is not only with the overt deed but also with the character of the doer; the humanity and tragedy of the malefactor are recognized no less than the hurt and wrong suffered by his victim. Thus we find in the Mishna that if one steals a beam from his neighbor and builds it into a home, the owner may not demand the return of the original beam. To put the thief to the expense of razing the home he had constructed might deter him from repentance. He is liable only for its monetary value.

The purpose of the laws of the Torah, declared a noted sage, is to refine man. Another outstanding legal scholar stated, "He whose wisdom exceeds his deeds, to what may he be compared? To a tree of many branches but few roots, which the wind can easily pluck up and overturn. But he whose deeds exceed his wisdom, to what may he be compared? To a tree of few branches but many roots which, even though the strongest wind blow upon it, will not be moved."[3]

The Rabbis saw the prescriptive law as the best means of introducing, through discipline and daily obligations, higher motivations and loftier purposes into the consciousness of man. Through deed, the will is mobilized and fortified. Even if one do a good act out of an unworthy motive, says an ancient teacher, he will, if he persists, come to be governed by a right motive. An admiring non-believer once said to Pascal, "I wish that I had your faith so that I might lead a life like yours." Pascal replied, "Lead my life and you will acquire my faith."

How ethical purpose mingled with legal decision is illustrated in the following two of many instances from the Rabbinic law that could be cited.

The Mishna states:

"A man may not go out bearing a sword or a bow or a shield or a club or a spear (on the Sabbath); and if he did he is liable to a sin-offering." Rabbi Eliezer says "They are his adornments" (they are really part of one's apparel and no penalty should apply). But the sages say, "They are naught but a reproach for it is written, 'And they shall beat their swords into plowshares and their spears into pruning hooks: nation shall not lift sword against nation, neither shall they learn war any more'" (Isaiah 2.4).

Interpreters of Rabbinic law point out that the difference of view reflects opposing social and economic classes. Rabbi Eliezer speaks as a patrician for whom the sword is part of festive dress, while his opponents are the spokesmen of the plebeians for whom a sword is a weapon and nothing more. The interest of this passage from the Mishna is by no means exhausted by this interpretation. We must not overlook the fact that the sages, whose position here is the accepted one, invoke in defense of their legal view that these objects may not be carried on the Sabbath, not a legal precedent or argument but a prophetic vision. The Scriptural support they employ is an Isaianic prophecy concerning "the end of days," in other words, a Utopian hope. Yet it is upon such a verse that they base their decision for the proper conduct in their day. Great law functions within sight of great goals, however Utopian they may appear at the moment.

The following is from the tractate dealing largely with court procedure:

> How did they instruct witnesses in capital cases with the enormity of their responsibility? They said to them, "Perhaps you will be inclined to testify on the basis of supposition, hearsay and by reliance on another whose word you regard as trustworthy. Remember, you will be closely examined. A criminal case is not like a civil one. In civil cases a man who gives wrong testimony may make atonement by payment of money. It is not so in criminal cases. The witness is answerable for the blood of the accused (who is wrongfully condemned by his testimony) and for the blood of his posterity (that would have been born to the condemned man). With regard to Cain who slew his brother, the Bible says "the voice of the bloods of your brother cry to me." Note the plural is used,

not blood, but bloods. The meaning is that Cain shed the blood of his brother and of his unborn posterity. Therefore did God create but a single human being to teach that he who slays a single soul it is accounted as if he caused the whole world to perish; and conversely, if a man saves a single soul, he is credited with saving the whole world. Another reason why God created a single human being was His desire for peace so that none should say to his neighbor "my father was greater than your father." Still another reason why God created a single human being was to proclaim the greatness of the Holy One, blessed be He. Man stamps many coins with a single die and they are all identical, but the King of Kings, the Holy One, blessed be He, stamped every man with the seal of the primal man yet not one of them is like his neighbor. Therefore each man may say "for my sake was the world created."

As Milton Steinberg comments in his *The Making of the Modern Jew*, this passage "reveals clearly the penetration of the law by moral idealism — a penetration in this case to the point of interruption and intrusion."

As new circumstances arose and men grew in their ethical sensitivity, the Rabbis were able by the process of interpretation to keep the law abreast of developments in social life, in intellectual comprehension and in moral perception. The Torah was a living law, deepening and expanding, responding to new needs. The Halacha served both as an instrument of communal cohesion and of moral discipline and education in the life of the individual.

Herford well expresses the achievements of the Rabbis in making of the Halacha the controlling factor in the life of their people. He writes, "What they did is surely one of the greatest attempts ever made in history to bring the actions of men into close relation with the sense of duty and their belief in God."

Let us pause for a brief examination of the method employed by the Halacha. We have already indicated that every word of Scripture was studied. Every stylistic peculiarity, an unusual word, a superfluous prefix, the repetition of a phrase or verse suggested that the verse had greater meaning than was apparent on the surface. We have two schools of thought among the Rabbis with regard to the degree to which the text is to be subjected to what has been described as "atomistic exegesis." A "loose construction" approach was characteristic of the school of Rabbi Ishmael. Since the Bible was intended for men, it was couched in language appropriate to men. Men allow themselves some latitude in written and oral communication and do not wish to be held to a rigid literalism. Rabbi Akiba and his disciples disagreed. One does not apply to a divine text the same standards by which one measures a human work. In Scripture there can be no stylistic lapse, no unintended circumlocution, no accidental repetition. Each word, indeed each letter, has a meaning which must be probed. This school of "strict construction" derived laws from prepositions, conjunctions, prefixes and suffixes.

A number of specific rules, generally referred to as hermeneutic principles, were formulated to discover the intent of the Biblical content. We know of seven such rules attributed to Hillel. Rabbi Ishmael drew up thirteen rules while Rabbi Eliezer compiled thirty-two principles of interpretation. We have room to cite but a few of these rules. The most common is "kal va-homer," arguing from the minor to the major and from the major to the minor. Work, for example, that may not be done on any other festival is certainly prohibited on the Sabbath, which is the holiest of occasions and to which, therefore, the more severe restrictions would apply. Conversely, any act permitted on the Sabbath is unquestionably permitted on the other festivals. Where the Bible states a general principle, it is to obtain in the case of instances which it patently includes, though they are not specifically enumerated. An example of this rule which may be cited is found in the Biblical law which prohibits one from taking a handmill or an upper millstone in pledge for a debt "for he taketh a man's life to pledge" (Deuteronomy 24.6). There can be no doubt, say the Rabbis, that the Bible is intent upon forbidding as a pledge anything needed by a man in preparing food for himself or his family. However, when a generalization is followed immediately by several specific instances, it is obvious that the principle applies only to the cases explicitly mentioned. Another rule was that if two verses seemed to contradict each other, a third verse would be found to reconcile the contradiction. The proximity of two sections afforded opportunities for drawing conclusions, which this proximity was taken to imply. Biblical law, for example, prohibits all labor on the Sabbath yet fails, as we have seen, to specify the kinds of work that are forbidden. The Talmud drew up a list of thirty-nine prohibited activities based on the work done in connection with the construction of the Tabernacle, since we find that Scripture deals with these two subjects — one close upon the other in several instances. From this textual proximity the principle is adduced that the work involved in the building of the Sanctuary is identical with the work prohibited on the Sabbath.

These and other rules of interpretation brought about the continuing expansion of the Halacha and the possibility of its application to new developments.

The Halacha grew and expanded in accordance with rule and method. The Aggada, which is that current in the "sea of the Talmud" which is non-prescriptive and non-legal, flowed far more freely. Here imagination and poetic insight ruled. Here we have the free play of the fantasy of individual teachers and of the folkmind. The lore of the Talmud reflects a high degree of creativity. It flies where the law strides. It leaps where the law walks. Zunz, the father of modern Jewish scholarship, describes the Aggada in this manner, "The Aggada, whose aim is to bring heaven nearer to men and again to lift men up to heaven appears in this mission as the glorifying of God and the comfort of Israel. Hence religious truths, moral lessons, discourse on just reward and punishment, inculcation of the laws in which the unique nationhood of Israel is manifested, pictures of the past and future greatness of Israel, scenes and stories from Jewish history, parallels between divine institutions and those of Israel, encomiums on the Holy Land, inspiring narratives and manifold consolation — these constitute the chief content of the synagogue homilies."

The eternal questions, the unanswered and unanswerable riddles of human existence, the expression of man's longing for God and his reverence before Him, wonder at the mystery of the universe, and even polemics with sectarians and heretics — all these and much besides has a place in the open field of Aggada. Every literary form is represented in it, the poetic image, the narrative, the light story, the thoughtful reflection, epigram, parable, allegory, biography, anecdote, the homiletical exposition. Aggada is not so labelled in the Talmud nor is it set apart from the legal discussion. It enters as an interpolation or is brought in as a diversion. A sage engaged in an intricate legal analysis finds a moment's release for himself and a rest for his disciples as he leads them from the highway of Halacha to a pleasant bypath of the Aggada. Aggada claims no authority for itself external to its intrinsic interest and fascination. One might, without any intention to be disrespectful, call it the play-life of the Rabbis, with the added note that it was the play-life of mature, ethical and spiritual men.

Everything lives in the Aggada. Nothing is permitted to remain inanimate. Not only are animals endowed with the gift of speech and the capacity for (and indeed love of) argumentation, but even hills and seas, the skies and the bushes, earth and the stones are articulate. Indeed even the letters of the alphabet hold forth with surprising volubility. The Aggada humanizes all that it touches and infuses all nature with consciousness. Neither the heavens nor He who dwells therein are beyond the reach of the Aggada. Without irreverence, it has God speak with the tongue of men and engage in the actions (though not, of course, in the sins) of man. The large folk element in Aggada and the free play of the imagination which it fosters have brought into this lore occasional elements of superstition and demonology.

Some citations will indicate something of the method and content of the Aggada though we cannot even begin here to suggest the scope and variety of this great and vital body of Jewish lore.

(On the basis of a fanciful interpretation of Isaiah 56.1, it was said that God recites prayer. And what is the nature of His prayer?)

God prays:

May it be My will that My compassion overcome My anger and that it may prevail over My attribute of justice and judgment, so that I may deal with My children according to the quality of mercy.

* * *

Slander slays three persons: the speaker, the listener and the object of its calumny.

* * *

Even the beggar who is supported by charity must practice charity.

* * *

When a pauper stands at your door, the Holy
One, blessed be He, stands at his right hand.

* * *

Man will be called to account for all the permitted
pleasures which he failed to enjoy.

* * *

(The dignity and sanctity and worth of the individual are constantly stressed and expressed in multiple
forms by the Aggada.)

Beloved is man for he was created in the image
of God.

* * *

One man outweighs all creation.

* * *

He who humiliates his fellow-man publicly, it is
accounted to him as if he spilled human blood.

* * *

He who strikes his fellow strikes, as it were, the
divine Presence.

* * *

Wherever you come across a footprint of man,
God stands before you.

* * *

(Aggada, on the other hand, is not unaware of man's
propensity for sin, of the dark forces that rise within him to assert themselves over him. Nor are the

sages unmindful of the pathos of man's frailty and mortality.)

All that God created in the beginning stands in the need of perfecting — not excluding man.

* * *

The evil impulse leads a man astray in this world and testifies against him in the next. The evil impulse within man seeks to restrain him from charitable acts by saying, "Why practice charity and reduce your possessions? Rather than give to strangers, give to your children." "There shall be no strange god in thee" (Psalm 81.9). Which is the strange god in man? It is the evil impulse.

* * *

The word "good" in the Biblical verse "And God saw everything that He had made and behold it was very good" (Genesis 1.31) includes the evil as well as the good impulse. But, it is asked, how can the evil impulse be termed "good?" The answer is, "Were it not for that impulse a man would not build a house, marry a wife, beget children or engage in trade." "Thou shalt love the Lord thy God with all thy heart" (Deuteronomy 6.5) means with two impulses (hence with *all* thy heart). Even the evil impulse can be used in the service of God.

* * *

It was a favorite saying of the Rabbis of the Academy at Jabneh, "I am a creature of God and my neighbor also is His creature; my work is in the city and his in the field; I rise early to my work, and he rises early to his. And he cannot excel in my work, so I cannot excel in his work. But perhaps you say, 'I do great things and he does small things.' We have learned that it does not matter whether a man does much or little, if only he direct his heart to heaven."

* * *

We can best summarize this chapter on Law and Lore in the words of a Jewish scholar of the last century.

It was the province of the *Halacha* to build upon the foundation of Biblical law, a legal superstructure capable of resisting the ravages of time, and, unmindful of contemporaneous distress and hardship, to trace out, for future generations, the extreme logical consequences of the Law in its application. To the *Aggada* belonged the high, ethical mission of consoling, edifying, exhorting and teaching a nation suffering the pangs and threatened with the spiritual stagnation of exile; of proclaiming that the glories of the past prefigured a future of equal brilliancy, and that the very wretchedness of the present was part of the divine plan outlined in the Bible. If the simile is accurate that likens the *Halacha* to the ramparts about Israel's Sanctuary, which every Jew was ready to defend with his last drop of blood, then the *Aggada* must seem "flowery mazes of exotic colors and bewildering fragrance," within the shelter of the Temple walls.[4]

VIII

WHO WERE THE RABBIS?

The Talmud bears the stamp of those who created it. We can understand the work better if we know more about those who formed and fashioned it. The Rabbis of the Talmud were not professional educators or ministers of religion as these terms are understood in our time. Their function is already indicated in a maxim attributed to the Men of the Great Assembly who were their forerunners, "Be deliberate in judgment, raise up many disciples, and make a fence about the Torah" (Abot I.1). Professor Moore points out that this statement embraces the three spheres of activity in which the sages were primarily engaged. The Rabbis served as judges, called upon to render decisions in the cases which litigants brought before them. They were therefore cautioned to develop a judicial temperament and to resolve controversies only on the basis of calm reflection. They were scholars expected to surround themselves with many students whom they were to train as their successors in scholarship and leadership. But the Rabbis also were the trustees of a tradition, the stewards of a sacred system of belief and behavior. The Torah was meant to be a guide for the life of the entire community. Consequently they were urged to "make a fence about the Torah," to encircle the Torah with safeguards to keep it intact amidst the tides of circumstance and the pressures of life.

While, as we have pointed out, the Rabbis did not regard themselves as innovators, they were not mere preservers and custodians of a system, finished and whole. They stood in the very midst of a process of growth and development, and they stimulated and directed the expansion and elaboration of the teachings they received. For them the law was an instrument for the enhancement of life and the elevation of man. It was a legal means to an ethical and spiritual end. They affirmed that the commandments were given so that man might be refined by them, for God is not affected nor concerned about the details of the law. The laws sought to inspire an ever present environment fostering man's spiritual growth. Conformity was not an end in itself. Indeed a time will come, as one sage stated, when men shall have so progressed that they will need neither the inducements to good nor the habituated restraints which the observance of the law helps to provide. The laws they dealt with were related to a view of the world and to an ultimate goal for man. Implicit in the activity of the Rabbis is an abiding faith, a profound commitment and a spiritual purpose. Despite their concern with matters of law, they were primarily men of the spirit.

The Rabbis were not by any stretch of definition philosophers. They did not construct an architecturally complete and coherent system of thought. Do not look in the Talmud for a structured exposition of a viewpoint moving from premise through inference and deduction to conclusion. A distinguished Biblical scholar who noted the same lack in the prophets explained the absence of an explicit philosophy in their writings by affirming that the prophets were too busy reacting to the thrill of the world to formulate a theory of the world. This explanation also applies to the sages of the Talmud. The Men of Sinai were not Olympian in their detachment. They were not scholars weaving their thought in intellectual retreats "far from the madding crowd's ignoble strife," aloof from "the actions and passions" of their times. The philosopher is essentially an aristocrat, standing at a remove from life, the better to view it. He sacrifices proximity for perspective and thus insulates himself against involvement. He is intent, as a modern thinker expressed it, upon preserving the chastity of intellect. The Rabbis, though their heads were often turned heavenward, stood firmly on the ground which they shared with their contemporaries. No barriers intervened between them and the community. They were in and of society and their teachings and decisions reflect the intensity and multiplicity of their attachments to it. The philosophy of the Rabbis is not organized as a system. It is implicit in their teaching and personal behavior. Dr. Max Kadushin has persuasively argued the organic unity which links the variety of their reflections and teachings into a coherent whole.

Many of the Rabbis gained their livelihood from worldly occupations. Serving as artisans, blacksmiths, sandal-makers, potters, grave-diggers, farmers, men of commerce, and tailors, the Rabbis were in touch with the pressures and currents alive in the community. Imbued with scholarly curiosity, their interest reached out into what we would today call secular interests and studies. Men of affairs, they had to be conversant with the world beyond their texts. They branched out into "worldly" sciences and studies not only the more effectively to interpret and apply the Torah but also because they considered all knowledge a revelation of the greatness of God and a manifestation of the wonder and beauty with which He filled the universe He had created. Anatomy was involved in many of the laws dealing with ritually fit and unfit animals and fowl. An early Christian father complained that the Jewish sages spent much time in the clinics of the physicians of the day. Neither was astronomy irrelevant, since in ancient times the sages determined the correct dates of festivals and established the calendar. One of the great Babylonian teachers testified about himself that he was as familiar with the heavens as with the streets of his native city. Whole sections of the Talmud deal with laws that presume a knowledge of botany and zoology. Many of the Talmudic scholars were masters of several languages and were versed in the history of the peoples about them. They responded to a lively interest in "the heaven above and the earth below."

The Rabbis gave the community visible instruction in the good life. Their acts no less than their lectures afforded instruction in the "ways of Torah." The leadership pattern they helped imprint upon the consciousness of the people was one characterized chiefly by intellectual, spiritual and ethical attributes. To be sure, one hears of Rabbis who betray an excessive pride in their eminence; others who are quick to anger and given to a sharp retort; one who though wealthy was parsimonious; one who became a heretic; some who behave with condescension to the unlearned. It is a tribute to the honesty of the Talmud that it includes these less pleasant accounts of some of the teachers, refusing to expunge them in the interest of self-glorification. The Rabbis, however, as a type of leadership and a class of men, embodied the values they sought to impart as teachers.

It is not easy to reconstruct the preparation a sage had to undergo in order to achieve recognition as a teacher. The institution of higher learning was known as Beth-Hamidrash — the house of study. The fact that the term is found in Ecclesiasticus (the Book of Ben Sira), one of the books of the Apocrypha, indicates an early origin for this school of advanced study. We find the term *Bet Va'ad Lahachamim*, a meeting place of scholars and disciples, on the lips of a teacher living in the 2nd century B. C. E. The student undoubtedly attended such a school for many years and sat at the feet of a distinguished master. Daily he listened to lectures until he had acquired sufficient knowledge to participate in the discussion that followed the presentation by the head of the academy. We have no way of knowing the length of time devoted to such preparatory instruction, but it is reasonable to assume that it lasted for a prolonged period. The biography of Rabbi Akiba gives some indication of the length of the period of training that was followed. Rabbi Akiba came from poor and unlearned stock. He married the daughter of a wealthy patrician, and was inspired by his wife to seek knowledge. According to the Talmudic account he was forty when his formal education began. Unabashed, he sat alongside of small children and diligently absorbed instruction in the alphabet and other subjects of the elementary curriculum. He left his wife and children for twelve years to become the student of an Academy and ultimately the most distinguished scholar of his age.

The collapse of Jewish national life stimulated rather than checked the will to disseminate knowledge of the Torah and led to organization of new academies. Professor Ginzberg cites the observation of Josephus written not long after the catastrophe of 70 C. E., "For though we be deprived of our wealth, of our cities or of the other advantages we have, our Law continues immortal." Rabban Johanan ben Zakkai established a school at Jabneh. Toward the end of the first century outstanding academies existed at Lydda, Bene-Berak, Peki'in and other places. Just as the effectiveness of the work of the Men of the Book in the earlier centuries was dramatically proved by the remarkable spirit of loyalty and resistance with which the Jews under the Maccabees met the attempts of Syria to destroy their religion, the enduring impact of the achievements of the Rabbis is evidenced by the fact that, while Hadrian during his religious attacks in the 2nd century C. E. killed many Jews, he was unable to achieve his primary aim of destroying Judaism.

In the third century great academies arose in Babylonia. The founder of the first great school was Rab who had studied in Palestine under Rabbi Judah Ha-Nasi. It was probably as a student — revealing that students will be students whether in Palestine or Harvard, in the third century or the twentieth — that he was nicknamed Areka, the tall one. Babylonia was at this time, in the words of the Talmud, "an open and abandoned field" which Rab proceeded to "fence in" with Torah. Rab established a school at Sura. Another academy was located at Nehardea and was headed by Samuel, who likewise was an alumnus of Palestinian schools. Samuel was both a physician and astronomer and excelled in the elucidation and interpretation of civil law. Rab, in addition to being a distinguished scholar and educator, was a man of genuine piety who composed prayers that still have a prominent place in Jewish liturgy, such as the Alenu prayer which closes every public service during the year, and the prayer that is chanted on the Sabbath preceding a new month.

The Rabbis were teachers of Torah, arbiters of controversy, and religious leaders. But they also were men of affairs who wielded great influence in determining policy and action. Rabbi Akiba was one of the leaders of the rebellion against Roman rule and met a martyr's death (135 C. E.).

Rabbi Akiba was not the only martyr. Rabbinic sources give us an account of nine of his colleagues who challenged the Hadrianic edicts forbidding the teaching or practice of the Jewish faith. Rabbi Judah ben Baba, one of this number, fled to a remote place, and there among the mountains ordained five disciples, Rabbis Meir, Judah, Simeon, Jose, and Eleazar ben Shamua. It was prohibited under pain of death to confer the title of Rabbi on a disciple, for the Roman Emperor was determined to break the chain of continuity of the tradition. Rabbi Judah ben Baba was apprehended and executed. Another sage was on the point of despair and feared that the evil empire would succeed in its avowed purpose. However his faith prevailed, for when his students asked, "Rabbi, what will our end be?" the master replied, "Cling one to the other, love peace and justice — there still may be hope."

This martyrology, which is incorporated in the service of Yom Kippur, not only evidences the heroism and determination of the sages in one of the most perilous and crucial periods of Jewish history, but symbolizes the nature of the Rabbis' active leadership at all times. This tradition continued through the centuries, and the Rabbi in medieval and modern life was the community's central personality as the school and synagogue were its primary institutions.

IX

THE RELIGION OF THE RABBIS

The term "religion" arouses certain associations in the mind of Western man: a particular edifice, a church; a day of worship, Sunday; a class of men, the clergy; a body of doctrines; memorable moments in one's own experience, confirmation, marriage or the funeral of a near one. What we have in mind in speaking of the religion of the Rabbis is an outlook upon life, the central source of their motivations, the dynamic convictions that were reflected in all they did. It has often been pointed out that neither Biblical nor Talmudic literature contains a concept which corresponds to our English word "religion." The Hebrew terms commonly used for religion do not accurately convey the meaning it has for English-speaking peoples. "Emunah" means faithfulness, dependability, trustworthiness. The other word generally used is "Dat," which in its classic context has no theological associations at all. Its meaning is a decree, command, royal edict. It is literally impossible in Judaism to isolate an autonomous religious aspect from the whole range of Jewish culture. The religious spirit pervades the entire tradition. Perhaps we can best suggest the essence of the term religion by the term Torah, though here too we are far from setting up a simple equation.

In the Greek translation of the Bible known as the Septuagint, the word Torah is rendered as *nomos*. *Nomos*, in classic Greek, had a wider meaning than the word "law" which has become its equivalent in modern translations of the Bible. Volumes could be written to describe the dust-storms of error and fallacy for which this inaccurate rendition is responsible. Torah is a basic concept in Judaism; to misconceive its full meaning is to misjudge Judaism. The Rabbinic world-view must be expounded in a way consistent with its own premises and terms of reference.

The basic convictions of the Rabbis revolved about the existence and attributes of God. Biblical and Rabbinic Judaism is saturated with an impassioned awareness of God's being and presence. The existence of God was not a reasoned conclusion resting on investigation and intellectual analysis. It was, therefore, neither philosophical nor scientific. The tradition was instinct with an intense emotional consciousness of God. Nowhere in the Talmud do we find an organized effort on the part of the Rabbis to "prove" what their lips proclaimed and their lives affirmed. It was not till later, when Judaism was challenged by the philosophers about it, that we find its thinkers attempting systematic formulations. The Rabbis were, however, too acutely intelligent not to find evidences in the world of nature and of reason pointing to a Creator. Rabbinic literature contains intimations of the arguments theologians and philosophers were later to organize and refine. A Rabbinic parable tells of a man wandering in a wilderness who came upon a large mansion. "Can it be," he asked, "that this edifice is without builder and master?" The owner soon made his appearance and disclosed his identity. Even thus was it with Father Abraham. He saw the world and deduced that it had a master. Yet it cannot be said that the belief in God was for the Rabbis the apex of a process which led to Him step by step. The tradition starts with a vital conviction that God is. As George Foot Moore puts it, "Its origin (i. e. the concept of God among Jews) was thus, to put it in a word, moral rather than physical or metaphysical; and it was therefore essentially personal."[1] The concept of God which the Hebrew distilled out of his moral and spiritual experience had, as Rabbi Silver points out, "an intensity of feeling, a passionate earnestness and a prophetic missionary zeal about moral values . . . which find slight parallel in Greek thought. Greek religious teachers did not 'hunger and thirst after righteousness,' though they sought earnestly to understand it and define it."[2]

We do not find in Rabbinic literature polemical discussions with those who completely deny the existence of God. Atheism and philosophical skepticism belong to a later day. The Rabbis, however, directed their shafts at those who accepted the existence of God but denied to Him the role of Judge of human actions and rejected the doctrine of retribution. For the Rabbis, being teachers, jurists and communal leaders, found themselves waging not an ideological battle on the plane of theory, but a struggle that continued from prophetic days, against immorality, social evil and wickedness within and without their community. They opposed those who lived as if *let din v'let dayyan*, "there is neither judgment nor judge in the world." A philosopher asked one of the Rabbis, "Who is the most hateful person in the world?" The sage quickly replied, "The man who denies his Creator." Pressed to explain, the Rabbi elaborated, "Honor thy father and thy mother; thou shalt not murder; thou shalt not commit adultery; thou shalt not steal; thou shalt not bear false witness against thy neighbor; thou shalt not covet — behold, a person does not repudiate any of these laws until he repudiates the root from which they sprang (namely, God who ordained them), and nobody proceeds to commit a sinful act without first having denied Him who prohibited it."[3] The Rabbis read a man's theology in his habitual actions. In our day, as Erich Fromm has pointed out, religion has won wide acceptance in terms of its theory of life and systems of value but meets defeat on the field of the daily practices, mores and norms by which men live in our technological society.

In the Rabbinic view, intense stress is given to the unity and singularity of God. Their belief in His incomparable and indivisible oneness and soleness allowed of no compromise. The Rabbis selected the sentence known as Shema, "Hear O Israel, the Lord our God, the Lord is One," out of the thousands of Biblical verses and made it the great affirmation of the Jewish faith. Pointedly one of the sages comments, "An earthly king has a father, a brother, or a son. This is not the case with God. God says, 'I am the first, for

I have no father; I am the last, for I have no brother; and there is none beside me, for I have no son.' "[4] "All things in the universe," the Rabbis remark, "come in pairs — heaven and earth, the sun and moon, Adam and Eve, this world and the world to come — only God is One and alone in the universe."[5] The Rabbis frequently inveigh against the theory of *shetei reshuyot*, which holds that life is divided between two forces, the good and the evil. Though such a view provides a simple and comprehensible explanation for the presence of evil and suffering in the world, it does so at the expense of the indivisible unity of the Sovereign of the Universe and cannot therefore be too strongly condemned. The belief in the oneness of God is so fundamental that the Rabbis did not hesitate to say that he who repudiates idolatry is accounted a Jew.[6]

God's incorporeality is emphasized next to His oneness. The Bible and indeed the Talmud too abound in many anthropomorphisms, some of which offend modern sensibilities. The purpose of the Torah was to instruct men. It therefore had to speak in the language of men. Since language grows out of the experience and thought of men, it cannot transcend human experience and thought. The anthropomorphisms are never regarded as anything but figures of speech. While there is a danger in picturing God in human terms, it cannot be avoided if we are to speak of God at all in the face both of God's infinitude and man's moral limitations. However, a good consequence resulted from this fact for, as Dr. Schechter observed, the Rabbis went far in "the humanizing of the Deity and endowing Him with all the qualities and attributes which tend towards making God accessible to man."[7] Thus the Rabbis picture the Creator as wearing phylacteries, wrapping Himself in a Talit or prayer-shawl, studying the Torah and even offering prayer to Himself. God visits the sick, comforts the bereaved and helps to attend to the dead. While of necessity anthropomorphisms were employed in speaking of God, any type of physical representation was forbidden. The idea of an Invisible God was incomprehensible even to cultured members of other societies. When Pompey conquered Jerusalem in 63 B. C. E., he arrogantly made his way into the Holy of Holies in the Temple. This urbane Roman was astonished to find no statue or any other tangible representation of the deity in the sacred chamber. He regarded the Jews as a superstitious and barbaric people.

While their manner of speaking of God brought Him somewhat nearer to the comprehension of men, the Rabbis emphasize the unbridgeable gap that intervenes between the divine and the human in majesty, power and essence. Man's capacity is not to be likened to God's capacity. When Moses asked that God reveal His "glory" to him (Exodus 33.18), meaning "the attributes with which God rules the world," God replied "Thou canst not comprehend My attributes." Man is not to presume to understand that which lies forever beyond his comprehension. The mysteries of life and of the universe are clear only to God. The human mind can grasp only a minute fraction of the grandeur, glory and infinite complexities that surround it. Does not Scripture say "In all thy ways know Him?" Note carefully "in all thy ways," not "in all His ways."

God's omnipotence is likewise celebrated. In the outlook of the Rabbis it is not merely prowess that is emphasized but rather the fact that God's might underwrites His law. No matter how vast and powerful earthly empires may become, it is divine justice that will prevail in the end. Professor Moore clearly summarizes this aspect of Rabbinic thought. "The almighty power of God was not in Judaism a theological attribute of omnipotence which belongs in idea to the perfection of God; it was, as in the prophets, the assurance that nothing can withstand His judgment or thwart His purpose. The omnipotence of God is thus interlocked with the teleology of history." [8]

The God of power, whose dominion is over all the world, is at the same time the Father who dispenses justice and shows mercy. Among men, say the Rabbis, he who rules by virtue of his power is not concerned with justice. In God alone are power and justice, might and mercy, united. The former is never displayed to the exclusion of the latter. The Rabbis cite Scriptural passages in which reference to God's power is followed by a reference to His humility. God the Father looms larger, so to speak, in Rabbinic theology, than God the Creator. When the Rabbis speak of God it is primarily with the thought of His relationship to His children and the revelation of His will in the Torah rather than in terms of the wonders, immensities and intricacies of nature. Nor is this mere human egoism.

For in God's scales too a single human being is not outweighed by all creation.

The conception of a God who is concerned about man represents a vast advance not only in theology but also in the entire range of man's relationship to the world of which he is part and in which he dwells. Early man looked out upon a world inhabited by malignancy, peril and uncertainty. He was at the mercy of powerful natural forces which he was not able to control. The gods whom he served ruled by caprice and recognized no limitation upon their will. Bound by no law, their actions were unpredictable. The worshipper never knew where he stood with those whom he worshipped. The universe as a result was a maddening chaos permitting no relaxation from fear and anxiety. The Homeric epics reveal the violence and lawlessness of such a world. One sought to propitiate the gods with every manner of sacrifice, not excluding human. While generally the gods may be presumed to look with favor upon those who brought them the fruit of their land, loins and livestock, there was no causal relationship between a man's acts and his gods' deeds. The gods, being amoral, were not constrained to recognize goodness or to reward virtue.

The entire background against which man moved and functioned underwent a radical transformation when he came to believe in a cosmic parent who was both just and loving. Ethical monotheism freed man from the bondage of terror. That God was just meant that a divine pattern rather than a potentate's whim ruled life. That He was merciful meant that God was not subject to malevolence or caprice. The Rabbis would understand the substance of Whitehead's definition of faith in reason, though he spoke in an idiom far removed from theirs. The modern philosopher spoke of a trust "that the ultimate nature of things lies together in a harmony which excludes mere arbitrariness." He is the God to whom Abraham could direct that statement which Zangwill described as "epochal," "Shall not the Judge of all the earth do justly" (Genesis 18.25). One of the sages, R. Levi, elaborates what he believes to be the implications of the patriarch's question. Abraham said to God, "If Thou desirest to maintain the world, strict justice is impossible; and if thou desirest strict justice, then the world cannot be maintained. Thou canst not grasp the cord at both ends at the same time. Thou desirest the world and thou desirest justice. Take one or the other. Unless thou art merciful the world cannot survive."[9]

The greatest duty man owes God is to follow in His ways and conform to His will. The principle of "*imitatio dei*," the emulation of the attributes ascribed to God, occupies an important place in Rabbinic thought. The Bible says "Ye shall walk after the Lord your God" (Deuteronomy 13.5). "How is it possible for man to walk after Him," the Rabbis ask, "Who is described as a 'consuming fire' " (Deuteronomy 4.24). The meaning is to incorporate in human life the qualities, so to speak, of the Holy One, Blessed be He. He is gracious, compassionate, slow to anger. He clothes the naked (Genesis 3.21); He visits the sick (Genesis 18.1); He comforts the mourners (Genesis 25.11) — man should do likewise.

The belief that man can on the human level follow the divine example implies a high tribute to human capacities and potentialities. The idea of original sin, namely, that the fall of Adam, the primal man, ineradicably infects every one of his successors — an idea that looms large in classic Christian doctrine — is not stressed in Rabbinic literature. The Talmudic view of man is more congenial. In addition, the Rabbis found in such an idea an infringement upon man's free will without which a moral life can have no meaning. In Judaism, "there is no notion that the original constitution of Adam underwent any change in consequence of the fall, so that he transmitted to his descendants a vitiated nature in which the appetites and passions necessarily prevail over reason and virtue while the will to good is enfeebled or wholly impotent."[10] To be sure, man is not without an inclination to sin. Scripture itself states that there is none so righteous that he sinneth not (Ecclesiastes 7.20). The "Yetzer Hara," the evil impulse within man often leads him astray. The Rabbis have a realistic awareness of the power of this impulse in the lives of men yet show a profound faith in man's capacity to direct and sublimate its energy in behalf of the good. Man's drives and passions are not to be suppressed or uprooted but rather restrained and guided by reason and morality. In modern parlance we would say that wholesomely sublimated, men's urges and impulses can serve as a source of creative energy. The Rabbis, opposing a dualism in the universe, were loath to assume a deep-cleft duality in man. Evil desires may have their origin in the will or mind but when man sins his body is not an unwitting accomplice. He sins as a unified, whole person, every part of whom is, in a sense, implicated in his misdeed.

The Rabbis were not unmindful of the coercive forces that play upon each man. Heredity, economic station, social conditions, health or sickness, strength or weakness, beauty or ugliness, wisdom or its lack are the results of circumstances beyond his control. The quality of his life — be it good or bad — rests entirely with him. "Everything is in the power of God — except the reverence for God by man." The Rabbis were likewise aware of the contradiction between God's omniscience and his consequent fore-knowledge of the future, and man's freedom of choice. They saw this contradiction as incapable of being resolved by human reason. What appears contra-dictory to man may be resolved in an intelligence higher than his. The great Rabbi Akiba gave the classic statement of Judaism's view on this matter. "Everything is foreseen, yet freedom is given; the world is judged by grace, yet all is according to the amount of good works."[11]

Man is not the puppet of the forces of history on the one hand, nor is he without self-determination before God, on the other. He plays a decisive, indeed the decisive role in his salvation. God's omnipotence does not presuppose man's nullity. It is man's will and decision that win him God's forgiveness, for he is not the passive object of divine grace. He is a partner in the process which leads to redemption. If forgiveness is the expression of God's love, man must merit it. Not stamped ineradicably with sin, man is possessed of the capacity to overcome the evil in him and the world. His triumph over sin becomes God's opportunity to extend forgiveness. Man thus serves, to use a phrase beloved of the Rabbis, as a *shutaf*, a partner and co-worker with God in effecting human regeneration and salvation, God creating by His presence the conditions of salvation, man achieving it by his will. Indeed, the Rabbis do not hesitate to assert that, in a manner of speaking, God needs man even as man needs Him. God suffers with them in their suffering and is with them in their distress. "If My people," says God to the angels, "decline to proclaim Me as king upon earth, My kingdom also ceases in heaven."[12] By a slight change of vowels, the Rabbis make the verse "I have brought you forth from Egypt" yield the meaning, "I (God) was brought forth with thee from Egypt."[13]

Existence is not a predicament but an opportunity to share in God's love and to advance His Kingdom upon earth. Salvation is not unearned, unrelated to human effort, a gracious gift of Heaven. It is the achievement of men in a world ruled by a God of justice and love. Redemption will not descend from heaven, it will be won on earth. Its source is not beyond history. Its stage is the arena where men live, struggle, aspire, worship, fail, suffer, repent and achieve salvation.

The Rabbis as heirs of the Psalmists and poets of the Bible were not unmindful of the beauty and harmony of nature. They introduced into the liturgy benedictions to be recited on seeing new blossoms in spring, on seeing the ocean, a rainbow, on hearing thunder and seeing lightning. To describe them as lacking in an aesthetic sense is to do them an injustice. Yet it was through the study of Torah rather than the study of nature that they achieved their most vivid awareness of God's presence and the most abiding feeling of their dependence upon Him. God as revealed in the Torah appeared to them more immediate, more majestic and more creative, in a manner of speaking, than the Creator who was manifest in nature. The Torah embodied, in their view, the divine design in accord with which the world was fashioned. In the Torah, you have the key to life and the universe. It was more than a fondness for rhetoric that prompted them to say that God had looked into the Torah before He began the work of creation. The plan preceded the world which was based upon it. Deeper than the order and regularity which characterize creation, more basic than its unity and beauty, testifying to the power of Him who fashioned it, is the underlying moral law upon which the Cosmic Lawgiver reared the structure which as Divine Architect He had designed. Such a law, while transmitted through one people, could not but be meant for all mankind. Hence the Torah was revealed in a desert, a place accessible to all nations, so that the Israelites could not deny to other people their rights to it. The divine voice at Sinai spoke in the seventy tongues then in use. Indeed the Torah had been offered to the other peoples. It was Israel's readiness unconditionally to accept and to live by it that determined its selection as the people of the revelation.

Leo Baeck points out in his *The Essence of Judaism* that neither in Biblical nor in Rabbinic writings does the term "good Jew" occur. It is the "good man" who is the subject of discussion and the object of concern. The concept of a God who rules over all the world, and of a moral law that is binding upon all mankind gave a universalism to the Jewish outlook which it could excise only at peril to its integrity as well as to its survival. It is possible to trace variations in the emphasis given to universalism in different periods of Jewish history. Persecution and deprivation sometimes drove the Jew to take refuge within himself and to shut out a mankind which seemed to be united upon his destruction. However, there always remained rooted with Judaism the larger view, the more comprehensive concern with the moral quality that should mark the life of all men.

Thus universalism and particularism united in the Rabbinic outlook. For such ages as would stimulate a narrowing of view, Judaism had a corrective in the concept of God and humanity which it embodied. For such ages, and there were some, that were prepared to lose themselves in a vague, diffused universal vision which left one free of imperatives and duties in the immediate present, there was the round of specific obligations and practice which would not allow one to surrender solid duty to airy hope. If the election of Israel implied superiority, it was a superiority that had to be paid for in service, suffering and sacrifice. If it brought added merit, it also brought added burdens. If it made one's people an instrument of prophecy, it also exposed it to a prophet's sorrow and fate. Within the doctrine which saw Israel chosen for a significant role in the drama of history, there were the polar elements of eminence and duty, greatness and steward-ship. They helped correct the extremes of arrogance and self-abnegation.

The treasure entrusted to Israel was meant for all mankind. To the Jew was given, as Milton Steinberg has expressed it, the secret of salvation but not its monopoly. "God has revealed it (the universal reli-gion) to one nation that through them it should be proclaimed to all the nations; Israel's exclusive posses-sion of it was not the end but the means to a greater end. The belief in the future universality of the worship of the one true God runs like a red thread through all the later literature, a day when 'The Lord shall be king over all the earth; in that day shall the Lord be one and His name one.' "[14] The verse cited occurs in the prophecies of Zechariah (14.9). That it was introduced by the Rabbis into the closing prayer of every public worship through the year, indicates its centrality in their thought.

The religion of the Rabbis was vitalized by universal faith and concretized by a specific and detailed regimen. In the Torah, God imbedded His deepest purposes and profoundest truths. Through study, reflection and diligent search, man both communes with God and releases and fulfills the most dynamic potentialities of his own growth.

X

ASPECTS OF RABBINIC SOCIAL TEACHING

A number of factors united to inform Rabbinic teaching with a deep social consciousness. First, there were the implications that flowed directly from a theology which made the attributes of God's justice and compassion paramount to His very existence. In Rabbinic literature, among the names applied to God are "Raḥmona," the Compassionate One," "Ab Ha-Raḥamim," "Father of Mercies," "Our Father in Heaven." Such is the love of God for His creatures, says a sage, that none may win His love who has not earned the love of his own fellows.

Secondly, the tradition that is embodied in the Torah abounds in legislation marked by social concern and obligation. When grain was harvested, corners were to be left uncut; sheaves dropped or overlooked were not to be gathered; vines and olive trees were not to be denuded completely. That which remained belonged to the poor (Leviticus 19.9, 10). The tithe of every third year was set aside for the needy of the community.

The most common word-combination in the Torah is probably "the stranger, the fatherless and the widow," and the most frequently rehearsed admonition is that which stressed the care and assistance due them. The Bible did not abolish slavery. It did, however, surround that universally accepted institution with humane restrictions. Torture, so common in the ancient world with regard to slaves, was unknown. Injury to the slave compelled his liberation. The Hebrew slave was to be released at the end of six years of servitude. Capital punishment was visited upon a master who killed his slave (Sanhedrin 71). The slave was to rest on the Sabbath and was to be included in the family celebration of festivals. An escaped slave was not to be turned back. Upon a slave's release he was to be granted liberal subsidies from his master's "flock, threshing floor and wine-press," so that he may have a foundation for a self-supporting life. For "Thou shalt remember that thou wast a slave in the land of Egypt" (Deuteronomy 15.12 ff. See also Joel 3. 1, 2).

According to Jewish law, no person is subject to duties but bereft of rights. Such an individual did exist in Roman law in the person of the slave. In the Hebrew concept, none, not the heathen slave nor the Hebrew, indeed not even the man condemned by law to death, was so reduced to a non-human status as to be without rights. In the strongest and most imperative terms are the Israelites commanded to aid the poor. The repetition of the Hebrew verb in the Biblical verse "patoah tiphtah" "thou shalt surely open thy hand to thy brother, to the poor and needy in thy land" and in the phrase "naton titen" "thou shalt surely give to him" indicates the importance of this obligation and the intensity with which the Bible projects it. The Rabbis however derived from Scripture more than legal direction and a basis for further elaboration. The social laws in the Bible are instinct with a profoundly humane spirit and this too was carried over into Rabbinic teaching. Moore thus formulates the relation of the Rabbis to the social legislation of the Torah, "Their task was therefore not solely to give a juristic definition of the statutes, with application to the various cases that were expressly or by implication covered by them, but to widen the scope of the law in accordance with its spirit and principle." The interweaving of spirit and statute, ethical ideal and legal enactment are characteristic of the Rabbinic approach.

Integral to the Biblical view was the passion for social righteousness which we tend to associate with the prophets. The Rabbis did not isolate the prophetic from the legal. The influences of both fused in the Rabbinic outlook. The result is a jurisprudence that is not only propelled by the precedent behind it but drawn by the vision of "the end of days" before it. The severe arraignments drawn by Isaiah and Amos, of a people that sold the poor into slavery and ground the faces of the needy; that set the widow, the fatherless and the stranger adrift; that substituted ritual for morality and preferred luxury to justice—this indictment coupled with the noble vision of a mankind living at peace and in security, imparted to the Rabbis a zeal that is felt even in the precise prose of their enactments.

A God-concept which gave preëminence to the divine attributes of justice and compassion, and a Book in which social duty was prominently embodied were fortified by a third force to influence the Rabbis in their interpretations. The tradition which they espoused was rooted in a community. A people rather than a class was to be its bearer. The arena for the fulfillment of the Torah was the life of the Jewish group, and the Rabbis habitually thought in terms of community rather than church. The individual soul could not be "saved" apart from the social body to which it belonged. Judaism was not meant for isolation and monastic withdrawal. The good life was that which was led in the midst of one's fellows, as one faced the trials and bore the burdens of interrelated living. "Separate not thyself from the community" was an oft-repeated teaching of the saintly Hillel which was re-echoed by other teachers. The absence of fellowship was equated with death by another sage. One's proper relationships with family, neighbor, employee were as much the content of the religious life as prayer, study and meditation. The concept "worldly" with the specific connotation and evaluation which it received in Christianity was absent from the thought pattern of the Rabbis; hence that which concerned men in their physical and economic life could not be ignored. The Talmud recounts that Rabbi Huna once asked of his son Rabbah why he did not attend the lectures of Rabbi Hisda who was noted for his wit. The son replied, "When I go to him, he speaks of mundane matters; he tells about certain natural functions of the digestive organs, and how one should behave in regard to them." His father replied, "He occupies himself with the life of God's creatures and you call that a mundane matter. All the more reason you should go to him."[1]

Israel Zangwill captured the accents of the Rabbinic tradition when he said that selfishness was the ultimate atheism. A faith socially-based and emphasizing practice above doctrine (the study of Torah was meant to culminate in the good deed) was bound to evolve a sensitive system of social legislation. The stress on social obligation, however, was not meant to negate or minimize the supreme value and dignity of the individual. The welfare of the individual and indeed his own inner development and fulfillment, to borrow modern terms, are best served by a society in which men are responsive to their duty one to the other. "He who destroys one life, it is as though he destroyed the entire world; while he who sustains one life it is as though he sustained the entire world."

The ties between men made each his neighbor's brother. In such a relationship responsibility was to be joined to personal regard for the object of one's ministrations. Not only was another's extremity not to become one's opportunity for gain, but another's need spelt no diminution of that cosmic dignity with which he and each of God's creatures were stamped. "When a beggar stands before one, God Himself is at his side."[2] One of the sages pointedly comments that Scripture does not state, "happy is who gives to the poor" but rather, "happy is who *considers* the poor" (Psalms 41.1). One's obligation is not discharged when one offers sustenance to the impoverished. One must not offend the sensibilities and self-respect of the recipient. One should consider the suppliant's rights as well as his need. The effects of the charitable act should not be vitiated by the inconsiderate spirit with which it might be administered.

The Rabbis would not have been happy with the uniform, minimal grants of assistance offered by public and private welfare agencies to their clients, though as realists they would have understood the need for such a procedure in our radically different society. He who speaks kindly words to the needy is more blessed than he who gives alms unaccompanied by kind words. Since the preservation of the dignity and self-respect of the recipient is essential, the Rabbis concluded that the man who lends is greater than he who gives alms, and that he who provides capital for a useful enterprise is greatest of all.[3]

Maimonides embodied the Rabbinic approach in his famous list of those who assist their fellow-men, drawn up in descending order of merit.

1. He who helps the poor by granting him a loan or by taking him into business.
2. He who gives to the poor without knowing him who receives and who remains unknown to the recipient.
3. He who gives secretly, hiding his own identity

from the beneficiary though knowing him whom he assists.

4. He who gives to an unknown recipient, but is known to him.

5. He who gives before being asked, the recipient and donor being known to each other.

6. He who gives upon being asked.

7. He who gives inadequately but with good grace.

8. He who gives with bad grace.

In Rabbinic times a hostel was attached to each synagogue, so that no wayfarer need remain without shelter. From the synagogue, honored and trusted collectors went forth weekly to solicit contributions for the support of the needy. The fund called *Tamḥui*, consisted of food and victuals, gifts in kind. Another fund called *kuppah* invited monetary donations. The poor of each town would receive aid every Friday, sufficient for a full week for themselves and their families. Clothing was distributed to the needy. Orphans were supported out of community funds. The community provided a dowry for poor or fatherless maidens. Free burial for the penniless was part of each community's responsibility. The most important fund of all, one which functioned till late in the Middle Ages and which dramatically reveals the perils which recurringly attended Jewish life, was *Pidyon Shebuyim*, the fund for the release of the captives. A moving history of the functioning of this fund in different periods and different lands could be written. (Read a most interesting account in Cecil Roth's *Personalities and Events in Jewish History*, in the chapter entitled "A Community of Slaves," pp. 112–135.) In times of stress all other communal needs were subordinated to the duty of freeing those held captive. The obligation to participate in the various endeavors for the needy rested, say the Rabbis, even upon an individual who was himself the recipient of public charity.

The Rabbis sought to imbue the life of the community and the consciousness of its members with the idealism of the Biblical prophetic tradition. The function they set for themselves was to transpose the great utterances and unique compassion of the prophets to the key of daily living. To give one example, the Rabbis interpreted the last part of Micah's summary of religion in terms of concrete applicability. "It hath been told unto thee, O man what is good and what doth the Lord require of thee, but to do justly, to love mercy and to walk humbly with thy God" (Micah 6.8). The Rabbis characteristically spell out in specific terms the phrase "walk humbly." It means, they said, the duty to join a funeral procession and by one's participation honor one whose life had come to its close. It means to attach oneself to the company that is escorting a bride to her wedding and help mark that important occasion in her life. The quiet, probably unnoticed sharing in a neighbor's joy no less than in his sorrow, constitutes an act of kindness. One famous teacher would call a temporary halt to study in the Academy when a bridal procession passed by the school saying "This deed merits priority over study."

The Talmud contrasts two approaches to the need of our fellow-men by means of a reputed conversation between Rabbi Akiba and Tinneus Rufus, the Roman governor. The Roman began by challenging the Jewish sage. "If your God loves the poor, why does He not provide for them Himself?" The Rabbi replied, "So that by reason of acts of charity we may be spared the punishments of the hereafter." The Roman persisted, " I do not see it in this light at all. The contravention of God's purposes merits punishment, not reward." The Roman sought to fortify his position with a parable. "A human king was angered by his slave and ordered him to be imprisoned without food or drink. Would it not be displeasing to the king if a commoner were to feed the slave?" Rabbi Akiba countered with a parable of his own. "A human king punished his son, placed him in prison and ordered that food and drink be denied him. A commoner, moved by the plight of the prince, fed him and gave him drink. When the king heard of this, his fatherly heart impelled him to reward his subject for his kindness to his son." The Rabbi proceeded to draw the moral of his parable. "We are children of God, as it is written, 'Ye are children of the Lord, your God.' " (Baba Bathra 10a). While the sage in this instance seemed to accept the Roman's premise that poverty is a penalty, his position that the poor too are "children of God" implies a social responsibility to the dispossessed which was entirely foreign to Roman society. In another place Rabbi Akiba states that even the poorest in Israel should be regarded as patricians who have come down in the world, for they are the children of Abraham, Isaac and Jacob. The Biblical verse, "deprive not the poor, merely because he is poor" (Proverbs 22.22), only apparently posed a paradox for how can one deprive the poor seeing that he has nothing? The answer of the Talmud is simple and direct, "Do not withhold from him what God has commanded thee to give him." The poor man might understandably surrender to bitterness and rebellion. He may cry out, "Why is my lot worse than other men's? Why do they have a home, why are their needs provided for, while I am homeless and uncared for?" "When one helps the poor," says God, "it is as if he reconciled the poor with Me and calmed their spirit."

While, as the Talmud declares, he who gives to the poor stores up treasures for himself in Heaven (a figure of speech which the New Testament borrowed), he is under no compulsion to impoverish himself by his charity. The sages were realistic enough to know that poverty can be as bitter as death. If a man gave with such abandon that he turned himself into a pauper and became dependent on others, what gain to society? The Rabbis would not agree with the advice Jesus once gave to a young man, "Sell all thou hast and give to the poor." A man's duty to the poor does not displace his duty to himself and his family. Altruism does not demand social self-destruction. A man should not give to charity more than a fifth of his possessions, the Rabbis declare. They also rule that a man should aid the poor of his own community before helping the indigent of other cities.

The Rabbis also expressed a profound concern with the rights of the laborer. The great principle of "Justice, justice shalt thou pursue" (Deuteronomy 16.20), and sensitivity to the rights of another informed Rabbinic extensions and supplementations of Biblical law. The Rabbis, rejecting the not uncommon contempt in which labor and the laborer were held in other societies, affirm that "no blessing rests upon a man except by the work of his hands." Indeed, they go so far as to state that he who enjoys the fruit of his labor is greater than he who fears the Lord. Rabbi Judah the Patriarch admonishes students to train themselves in a handicraft no less than in the Torah. A parent does not fulfill his duty to his son unless he teaches him a trade, since otherwise his son might fall into evil and dishonorable ways. A person should willingly do menial and even distasteful tasks in order to avoid being dependent upon his neighbors. A community should provide its citizens with the opportunity for honest work. The man who devoted his time to study was not to exalt himself above him who toiled in the field. The scholars of Jamnia were wont to say, "I am a creature, and he who is a worker is likewise a creature. My duties are in the city, his in the field. I arise early to my labors, he to his: Even as he does not mock my work nor seek my position, I do not regard his as unworthy. Lest one say of me that I do more than he, we have been taught, 'He who produces more and he who produces less are equal, as long as their hearts are directed heavenward.' "[4]

The Talmud, centuries in advance of general usage, sets a limit upon the hours which one may be required to work. Laborers were permitted to join together and set a wage scale which employers could be asked to meet. A workingman's tools were not permitted to be taken as security for a loan granted him. If taken, they had to be returned to him when he needed them for his work. Employers were not permitted to pay the wages of their workers in kind, so that the latter should not be exposed to the risk of receiving inferior goods appraised at inflated values. (Rabbinic ethics would prohibit the "company store.") In such instances where agreement stipulated that the laborer was to receive his meals, the employer was obliged to provide the best quality of food. A laborer's salary was not to be cut during the period of his absence by reason of illness.[5]

In the Rabbinic approach to labor, we thus find insights that had to wait many centuries for their acceptance. It would be idle to seek in Rabbinic literature solutions for many of the tensions that strain the relations between labor and management in our time or for explicit counsel in meeting such problems as automation, pensions, guaranteed annual wage, closed or open shop. The Talmudic view, however, would alert us to the two basic dimensions of this significant field, namely "the demands of justice" and "sensitivity to human needs, dignity and rights."

The laborer, on his part, may not be lax in his responsibilities. He should possess the skill requisite for the proper performance of his duties, so that he neither turn out inferior work nor by his ineptness cause financial damage to his employer. According to the Talmud, the laborer is liable for damage resulting from his inefficiency or carelessness.[6] The worker also is cautioned not to spend his leisure in a way to make himself unfit to meet the demands of his assignment.

In the larger sphere of the questions involving the power of government and the rights of the governed, we find Jewish tradition leaning to what would, in our time, be described as the democratic view. The national history of the Jewish people, as a people, began like that of the American, with a revolution. The impact of its origin exercised a significant influence upon its thought. Benjamin Franklin, in the early days of our Republic, suggested that the Great Seal of the new government depict the exodus of the Israelites from Egypt and that it bear the inscription, "Rebellion Against Tyrants is Obedience to God." The tradition of defiance of a king who equated might with right and who overreached himself in the exercise of his power, persisted. One need only turn back to the memorable Biblical descriptions of the prophet Nathan confronting King David with the accusation, "Thou art the man," and of Elijah hurling at Ahab the stinging words, "Hast thou murdered and thinkest thou also to inherit?" (2 Samuel 12 and 1 Kings 21). This tradition already has its inception in the Pentateuch which emphasizes the idea that the king is subject to the law. The concept "the king can do no wrong" could not find acceptance in the midst of a society which believed in God and not a mortal king as the source of law. It was inevitable that a people whose historical circumstances made it subject to the rule of foreign powers developed an awareness of the dangers and evils that inhere in an unjust government which recognizes no moral restrictions upon its power. All too easily could a government become fired by a zeal for domination and impose upon its subjects the heavy yoke of its unrestrained passion for power. The state could be subverted to the service of the few at the expense of the many. Yet the absence of government could result in anarchy with an attendant violence, second to none that any tyranny has caused. A sage casting perhaps an oblique glance at those who in their utter hatred of Rome and the oppression it brought, opposed all rule, admonished his hearers, "Pray for peace of government; for were it not for fear of it, men would swallow one another alive." (Aboth III, 2). There could be too little government, no less than too much. In the Jewish view loyalty to government could never be primary. Above government, as above all history, was God. Ruin awaited those mortal rulers who forgot that they, like their subjects, owed ultimate allegiance to God and His laws of justice and right. A government that made its own aggrandizement the sole criterion of its policy and which recognized no law above its own was a *malchut ha'reshaah* or *memshelet zadon*, a wicked and evil empire. Men who served mortal men, to the exclusion of God, were *avadim l'avadim*, "the slaves of slaves." Absolute power was never to be wielded by any government. A ferment of discontent, indeed of revolt when possible, should be kept alive in the hearts of men whose rights and dignities are trampled upon by unconscionable rulers who translate their will into law. "The rights of sovereignty" were always to be subject to the "sovereignty of rights."

Within the Jewish community, the law of the Torah was to be the guide of right policy and action on the part of those who were entrusted with leadership. Since knowledge of the Torah, due to the traditional emphasis on study, was never limited to those in official position, the acts of the leaders had to be justified to a constituency not unaware of the limitations on authority imposed by the basic law of the group. Leadership, as one Rabbi defined it to disciples whose modesty made them reluctant to accept communal posts of authority, was thus seen to be servitude rather than domination, an obligation to serve rather than an opportunity to lead. The true leader did not exceed the rights that were his; at the same time, he did not abdicate to his people when they sought that which was wrong or evil "in the eyes of the Lord." The Jewish community, to be sure, reflected on occasion the weaknesses which dog the steps of man's organized life. The rich often achieved a prominence not dictated by merit. Partiality and partisanship were not always absent. Two safeguards, however, served as bulwarks against the perversion of authority. One was a law, informed with a spirit of righteousness, which transcended local rule and which could be freely invoked; the other, a strong tradition of leadership which was qualified by reason of the two attributes of intellect and integrity, learning and personal character. The community's corporate life no less than that of the individuals who composed it, rested on a book and its manifold oral interpretations. A schooled and informed leadership was necessary properly to expound and apply such a tradition.

The differing conceptions of Roman and Jewish law concerning private property illustrate another aspect of Rabbinic social teaching.[7] In the former, property is a coefficient of power; ownership depends on occupancy or conquest and not on labor or moral right; in the latter, right is the determinant and neither occupancy nor formal ownership are decisive (occupancy is effective in case of unclaimed or ownerless property). Occupancy must be fortified and justified by a rightful claim. Labor constitutes an important element in possession. The term *kinyan*, meaning acquisition, is derived from a root connoting "to make."

Ownership, however, is never absolute. The court has the right to deprive a person of his property by declaring it ownerless, when the welfare of the community requires it. (This power of the court is known as *hefker bet-din hefker*.) Sometimes the reason given for the curtailment of the rights of ownership is *tikkun 'olam* — the general good. Bounds are imposed upon private ownership *mipnei darkei shalom*, in order to promote peace and preserve harmony. Property rights must yield to moral right and to human rights. The Talmud, by tracing back many restrictions upon private property to the days of Joshua bin Nun, when the land was distributed among the tribes, suggests that inherent in the conditions of ownership from the outset were a recognition and an acceptance of limitations. Thus the fact that a well found in a field privately owned was to be made available to the people of the town; the right of all to fish (with a hook and not a net) in the Sea of Tiberias though it was situated in the domain of the tribe of Naphtali — these and other similar curbs upon absolute ownership were implied in the original grant by which the people had received title to their land. Basic to Jewish law of property is the concept of moral and social limitations upon ownership.

The same principle is applied by the Rabbis to the world of trade. What is called by us "private enterprise" has a public aspect which should not be ignored. According to the Rabbis, profits, for example, should be subject to restraints. Profits on sales may not exceed one-sixth. Later commentators apply this restriction only to the articles that may be classified as "necessities." On less essential goods, a higher profit was to be permitted, while no ceiling was to be placed on profits in the case of luxuries.

Professor Samuel Atlas points out that this classification "is based on the general principle that the more an article is needed by the community, the less right has a person to make it an object of private gain, and the amount of profit allowed on an article is in inverse proportion to its usefulness to the community." Overseers were appointed by the court in Rabbinic times to prevent overcharges by unscrupulous merchants. There were communal inspectors of weights and measures. In Palestine, middlemen were not permitted to intervene between farmer and consumer in the instance of specified necessities, since their participation in the process of exchange would increase the cost. Communities had the right to peg prices of commodities at a maximum and to fix wages. Overcharge could be the basis for the cancellation of a sale. "Ye shall not wrong one another" (Leviticus 25.14) was taken to mean that if a sale represented a proved unfairness disadvantaging the seller or the purchaser (the latter paying too much or the former charging too little), it could be legally invalidated. Rare objects and other objects whose worth was based on personal evaluation rather than on that of the market were exempt from the limitations on price imposed by law.

Rabbinic social thought contains insights which have significant implications for our day, though it differs profoundly from the far less complex life the Rabbis knew. High moral values, a moving passion for right, a sense of mutuality and a deep sensitivity to the dignity of the individual, comprise a complex of qualities which characterize the Rabbinic outlook.

XI

ON JUSTICE AND
COURTS

The modern Jewish philosopher, Asher Ginzberg, who wrote under the pen-name of Aḥad Ha'am ("One of the People"), sought to establish the thesis in a famous essay that the central characteristic of Jewish thought and teaching is justice, which in the instance of Judaism transcended love and compassion. While this view suffers from the exclusiveness and subjectivism which mark any attempt at a monistic explanation of a multi-dimensional phenomenon, it properly stresses a value which the Jewish outlook enshrined as indispensable. Neither human life nor a religious interpretation are possible without it. Rabban Simon ben Gamaliel used to say, "On three things does the world rest, on justice, truth and peace."[1] The Scriptural basis of this dictum is the verse from Zechariah, "These are the things ye shall do: speak ye every man the truth with his neighbor, with truth, with peace and with justice, judge in your gates" (Zech 8.16). Appended too is the sublime comment, "And the three are one. If truth is wrought, peace is wrought; where justice is wrought, peace and truth are wrought also."[2] To pervert justice is to shake the entire world, for it is one of its foundations.

Rabbinic teaching goes into subtle and utopian

refinements where justice is concerned. Injustice is not limited to an act which inflicts injury or deprives one of his rightful possessions. By word or gesture we may perpetrate unfairness, even though the victim may be entirely unaware that he has been wronged. A man who knows evidence favorable to his fellow but withholds it may not be liable in a human court, but Heaven will punish him. A man must not urge his neighbor to dine with him when he knows that his neighbor is committed to another engagement and cannot accept his invitation. One must not ask the price of anything, in the absence of an intention to purchase, since he is unjust to the merchant whose hopes he falsely raises. In giving counsel to one who has sought it, one should not suppress any pertinent information or hide one's own interest if it be involved.

No evil-doer is the object of greater condemnation than the judge who violates his trust. He is, say the Rabbis, the cause of misfortunes which are visited upon the society which has elevated him. He not alone profanes the name of God but causes Israel to fall by the word and to be exiled from their land. On the other hand, we are told that, "To every judge who judges truly even for an hour, Scripture accounts it as if he had been a partner with God in the work of creation."[3]

Particular attention was given to the development and perfection of judicial procedures and practices which would act as safeguards against the perversions of justice. The judge was to be learned in law, yet no less a person of strong moral convictions, of deep religious faith and of unpurchasable integrity. The scales of justice were not to be tipped by awe of the powerful and wealthy, nor by sympathy for the weak and the needy. Probably every legal system admonishes its judicial officials not to favor the rich nor to yield to the influential. Such instruction is a staple of legal ethics. Scripture, however, warns judges in two different instances not to favor the poor (Exodus 23.3 and Leviticus 19.15). The Rabbis spell out the meaning of this principle, "When a poor man is one of the parties, the judge may not say, 'This is a poor man, and I and the rich man (who is the other party), are bound to support him; so I will acquit him in order that he may be supported as an innocent man,' therefore does Scripture warn 'thou shalt not favor the poor.' "[4] The point had to be stressed again and again, since a people trained in compassion could all too easily allow charity to determine what justice must decide. The Psalmist urges us, "Judge the poor and fatherless, do justice to the afflicted and needy" (Psalms 82.3). Note, the sages say, that this verse does not say "have pity on," but "do justice to." The judge should render righteous judgment whatever be the status of a litigant. As a private citizen, the judge may help the needy. In his judicial role, however, he must decide not on the basis of sympathy but of justice.

While the Jewish community was frequently ruled by foreign powers, it conducted its own internal affairs and maintained its own courts. Even under Roman rule, civil and probably criminal cases too, short of capital offenses, were dealt with in Jewish courts in accordance with Jewish law and procedure. The lowest courts consisted of three judges, superior courts of twenty-three and the Supreme Court of seventy-one judges. No man could incriminate himself. Testimony was not accepted from usurers or gamblers. Close relatives of the principals were likewise barred from testifying. Witnesses were interrogated separately. Every effort was made to impress upon them the full seriousness of their responsibility. Any discrepancy in the testimony of the witnesses automatically led to acquittal in a criminal case. For acquittal, a majority of one was sufficient; for conviction, a majority of at least two was needed. Circumstantial evidence was not acceptable. Where the penalty could be death, two witnesses, who could be cross-examined, had to see the crime. They were called upon to testify not only about the facts as they saw them, but also to the defendant's capacity to understand and know the meaning of his actions and their consequences. The defendant's moral responsibility had to be established before he could be convicted. The witnesses had to warn him about the serious nature of his act and the penalty which it brought on. His replies would have to indicate a full awareness of his actions. While Biblical law imposed capital punishment, the Rabbis hedged Scriptural legislation with so many qualifications and conditions that it could be said that Rabbinic law abolished the capital penalty. The Mishna severely castigates a court which pronounces a death sentence once in seven years, for the judges did not exercise sufficient care in their procedure to make the death penalty impossible. Rabbi Eleazar ben Azariah amends the Mishna to read "once in seventy years." Even so rare an instance of capital punishment deserves severe criticism. Rabbi Akiba and Rabbi Tarfon add that if they had been members of the court no man would ever have been put to death.[5]

When the judges after deliberating on the testimony were ready to render their opinion, they did so in the reverse order of their seniority. The youngest judge spoke first, and the oldest last. The purpose was to prevent the younger men, who may have been the disciples of the older, from being influenced by the views of their elders. Care was taken that each should render his independent judgment.

Once again it is evident that the rabbis, while judges and students of the law, did not cease to be ethical and religious spokesmen and teachers. A legal system seeks to conform to ethical standards and to embody high moral principles. However, a legal system also tends to achieve an autonomy which may lead it to develop in accordance with its own logic and precedents, detached from an ethical outlook, though not necessarily opposed to it. In Judaism no such separation took place. The law remained integral to the entire nexus of religious doctrine and spiritual aspiration. Behind the interpreter of the law stood prophet and moralist. The sanctions upon which the legal aspects of Judaism were based derived from the larger tradition. Disciplines which in our more complex day function with a high degree of independence were in the case of Rabbinic Judaism knit together in an organic unity.

XII

THE DENIALS OF
RABBINIC TEACHING

The Talmud is an arena of controversy, or to describe it perhaps more appropriately, a great academic lecture hall in which a debate is in progress. Yet spanning the differences of views and bridging the centuries during which the discussion continued, is a consensus. An organic unity underlies and indeed provides the sustaining foundation for the clash of views and interpretations. We have here a universe of thought, not simply a chaos of disagreement.

The individual sage is part of a group and his opinions are related to a cultural background which he shared with his opponents. All live within a tradition; their views, for all their specific deviations, have a basic unity. We have attempted to describe this basic unity in our exposition of Talmudic teaching on some of the fundamental themes with which it concerns itself. However, every significant affirmation involves denial. Every definition must exclude as well as embrace. In this chapter we shall seek to highlight a number of Rabbinic views by contrasting them with various concepts found in other cultures and faiths. Some of the elements in the Rabbinic consensus will thus be more vividly illustrated. Occasionally, a voice can be found in the Rabbinic tradition which concurs with the opposing position. However, the basic unity of Judaism, as it is reflected in the Talmud, is not shattered by the incidence of a solitary dissonance. In speaking of the Rabbinic view, I refer to the dominant stream of basic teaching which is recognizable despite the presence of occasional deviation.

I. *"Credo Quia Absurdum Est."* Tertullian, one of the early Church Fathers who taught in the early part of the third century, uttered the famous statement, "Credo Quia Absurdum est," "I believe that which is unreasonable." Aware of the inherent limitations of the human intellect, he refused to make reason the arbiter of truth. There is a higher truth, he claimed, the truth of faith, of revelation, of intuition. Logical consistency and intellectual validity are not the most significant attestations of truth. Something which appears untenable or even absurd to the mind may reflect a truth that reason, of itself, could never discover. He thus drew back from a dispute with the philosophers and philosophic systems which contradicted the faith he desired to propagate. He states, "We want no curious disputation . . . no inquiry after enjoying the Gospel." He called philosophers, "the patriarchs of heresy." He frankly asked for a suspension of reason and its critical faculties and a surrender to the creed he upheld. Other Church Fathers followed his approach and did not hesitate to term philosophy "a device of the devil." People who permitted their reason to be an obstacle to their faith were sinful men whose pride delivered them to Satan.

Among the Rabbis, there was a recognition that reason alone is not competent to solve all problems of a life that does not always conform to the canons of logic. However, the tradition does not dismiss reason lightly, nor does it disdain its use in the large areas of experience to which it is applicable. The human mind is not referred to with contempt, nor is unreasonableness elevated to a virtue. Rabbis opposed specific doctrines advanced by Greek philosophers but did not ban philosophic inquiry or learning as such. A non-Jewish student writing of the people that created the Bible says, "Creative skepticism was very much alive in this people." There are books of doubt and probing in this classic of faith. The Rabbis included Ecclesiastes and Job in the canon. The encounter of Judaism and philosophy in the Middle Ages (Saadia, Crescas, Maimonides) produced a notable chapter in the history of Jewish thought. The exaltation of learning as an indispensable condition of the religious life (Hillel said "an untutored man cannot be devout, nor can a man unlearned in Torah be saintly")[1] led to a stress on the development of the mind. Study was worship and enjoyed precedence over prayer. The chief function of the synagogue was to serve as a house of study. A benediction was to be recited upon seeing a scholar, be he Jew or Gentile. Rabbis delved in astronomy, botany and medicine. A saying current in Palestine in Rabbinic times, was, "He who has knowledge has all; he who has no knowledge what has he? He who has knowledge, what does he lack? He who lacks knowledge, what has he?"[2] The learned Gentile was to be honored above an ignorant High Priest.

The question is sometimes asked, in the course of a Talmudic discussion, why it is necessary to turn to Scripture for the basis of a rule that rests on common sense. The rabbis desired to protect what has been called "autonomy of Juristic thought," that is, the independence of legal development from considerations other than its own consistency and logic. A Rabbinic story best illustrates the jealousy with which the rabbis guarded the inviolability of their thought and of the legal process.

On one occasion Rabbi Eliezer used all the arguments at his command to justify his opinion. His colleagues refused to accept his view. "If I am right, may this carob tree move a hundred yards from its place." It did so. The Rabbis said, "A tree is no proof." Then Rabbi Eliezer said, "May the canal prove it." The water of the canal began to flow backwards. They said, "We accept no testimony from water." He then said, "May the walls of this House of Study prove it." The walls of the building tottered as if they were about to fall. Rabbi Joshua rebuked the walls, "If scholars argue about the Halacha, why do you intervene?" Out of deference to Rabbi Joshua the walls did not collapse, but neither did they become quite straight, out of respect for Rabbi Eliezer. Then Rabbi Eliezer said, "If I am right, let the heavens declare it." A heavenly voice was heard saying, "Why do you oppose Rabbi Eliezer? His view is right." Then Rabbi Joshua arose and said, "It (the Torah) is not in heaven." (Deuteronomy 30.12). What did he mean? Rabbi Jeremiah provided the explanation, "His meaning was that the Torah was given to man at Sinai. We do not regard a heavenly voice as binding. Did not the Torah state, 'You are to decide by a majority?' " (The verse in Exodus 23.2 is here interpreted homiletically.)

A note is added which may be regarded as an epilogue to this story and which makes its intent unmistakably clear.

The story proceeds to tell that Rabbi Nathan met Elijah the Prophet and asked him what God did during the incident in the Academy that has been described. Elijah replied, "He laughed and said, 'My children have triumphed over Me.' " [3] The use of reason by man evidences the divine image in which he was created.

The Rabbi was both a man of faith and a man of learning. His eminence as a spiritual leader and as religious authority rested on his learning no less than on his devoutness. Faith without knowledge would be a meaningless statement to the Rabbis. The intellectual element remained vital and powerful in the Jewish pattern. Mystic movements arose and occasional revolts against reason broke out. However, respect for reason in Judaism was too integral to be overcome. The Rabbis, by their own example, by their stress on study, by the hero-type they provided, and by the literature which they created and which remained the chief subject of the curriculum of Academies for centuries, helped keep Judaism intellectually vigorous and alert.

II. *"Extra Ecclesiam Nulla Salus."* A pupil of Tertullian, Cyprian, is the author of the doctrine that there is no salvation outside of the Church. It is impossible to render this statement into classic Hebrew because it deals with categories that are alien to Jewish thought. Jews do not constitute a church but a people. One of the reasons the modern Jew finds it difficult to define his identity is that the English language offers no term to suggest the complex of ethnic, national, cultural and religious elements that constitute the collective life of the Jew. The irreligious Jew is not read out of the community. Affiliation with the Jewish group is not a matter of creed. The religion of the Jew embraces areas that modern man would call secular. There is no instance, in the Western world, of an ethnic group whose religion emerged out of its own history. Hence the word "church" does not fit the Jewish situation. Nor is the word "salvation," freighted as it is with specifically Christian connotations, translatable into Hebrew. "Salvation" will be the merit of those who lead the good life. Thus "salvation" functions in Judaism in a far larger context than that of a creed or even of regimen of practices we term "religious." The non-Jew too has access to such "salvation." The Rabbis speak of *hasidei 'umot ha-'olam*, "the righteous among the Gentiles." Loyalty to the moral principles of the Torah, not membership in the group, made for righteousness. "I call heaven and earth to witness that whether one be a Gentile or an Israelite, man or woman, slave or handmaid, according to their deeds, will the Shechina rest upon them." ‘ The Scriptural verses that are invoked are "which if a *man* do he shall live through them," (Leviticus 18.5) and "This is the

Law of *man*." The Rabbis point out that the Bible speaks of *man*, not Jew.

The absence of a creed promising salvation and of a sense of monopoly in possessing it, led to a minimal preoccupation with heresy. Intolerant of idolatry, Judaism did not fashion a vise of dogma within which life had to be led. The statement "So far as heretics are concerned, heresy is a sin by which the offenders have deserved not only to be separated from the Church by excommunication, but also to be put out of the world by death" (Thomas Aquinas), could have no counterpart in Jewish literature. The nearest the Rabbis came to define the heretic is the dictum in Abot III.15, and it deals with wrong and immoral behavior rather than with doctrinal deviation. R. Travers Herford, in commenting on this statement, dryly observes, "If it (Pharisaism) affirmed that they (the heretics) had no part in the life hereafter, at least it did not cut short their life here." History deprived the Jew of the power to persecute those guilty of heresy. His tradition did not inspire a passion for such persecution.

III. *"Original Sin."* In Christianity there is a strong emphasis on the doctrine that man comes into the world tainted with a sin of which he cannot be cleansed by his own unaided efforts. Divine intervention is needed. Even in primers for the very young, there is likely to be an allusion to this concept. A rhyme that children learn, has it that

In Adam's fall

We sinned all.

According to St. Augustine, "The act of generation . . . is sin itself and determines the transmission *ipso facto* of the sin to the new creature." Every child inherits the guilt of the race at birth. All men are deep-dyed with this profound and ineradicable sin. Humankind is the prisoner of its own nature.

Hence man is completely dependent upon the mercy of God for his redemption. Neither his works nor his character can of themselves save him; only unmerited divine grace can redeem man. As Paul states in the Epistles to the Romans, "So it depends not upon man's will or exertion but upon God's will."

The concept of original sin plays no important role in Jewish theology. Isolated allusions to it may be found in the literature, but the fall of man gave rise to no fundamental doctrine and did not yield the idea of inherited guilt. Judaism rejected both the pessimism inherent in the idea that man is born in sin, and the fatalism that flows from such an idea, since man is rendered helpless from the start to effect "salvation" by his own efforts. A Christian scholar, Dr. James Parkes, summarizes the contrast between Judaism and Christianity in this respect, when he writes, "In Judaism, God says to man 'Fulfill my plan for creation'; and man replies: 'I will.' In Christianity man returns to God to say 'Fulfill Thy part in creation which I cannot because I am foolish and sinful,' and God replies, 'I will.' "

The daily prayers of the Jew include the affirmation "The soul Thou hast given me is pure." Man is not dogged by a sense of inhering sin. He permits his passions to overpower his judgment. He allows his will to capitulate to his senses. Possessing freedom of choice, he does not always choose the good but follows evil. But waywardness is no relentless necessity. Man need not submit to his own weakness. He possesses powers which if fostered and developed will enable him to live his life on a high plane of aspiration and achievement. The Rabbis find in the words in Genesis (2.3) "which God had created to do," a suggestion that God did not complete many of the elements in His creation, preferring that man perfect the undone. Man himself is incomplete. He is charged with the culmination of the process of creation begun by God. Man is therefore termed in Rabbinic teaching "shutaf l'Ha-Kadosh baruch Hu," "a co-worker with God in the act of creation." God in a manner of speaking is strengthened by His children for when they do His will they add to His power. [5]

Man's freedom is not curtailed by any irremediable defect in his nature. No determinism external to him predestines him to follow the path of sin and folly. In the range of choice open to him are good and ill. "See I have set before thee, this day, life and good, death and evil" (Deuteronomy 30.15). Man's redemption lies within his own power.

IV. *"My Country Right or Wrong."* This doctrine enjoys an acceptance belied by the frequency with which it is condemned. Nationalism has been termed the religion of modern man, and as a religion it confers ultimate validity and value upon its postulates. Many men, who might be hesitant to articulate their true feelings, consider their country's welfare as the supreme aim to which morality and justice are subordinate. We have advanced in our rhetoric to a point where we are ashamed to profess such a view, but in this respect as in others, our rhetoric has progressed beyond our motives. One of the crucial problems in our time is the tenacity with which nations hold on to their vaunted sovereignty as the final good when the interdependence of the peoples of the world demands a broader loyalty and a more moral goal. The nemesis that haunts human life is the pathetic fallacy which leads men to turn means into ends and instrumentalities into purposes. States and governments which should be means to human welfare and to world peace become canonized ends to serve which is man's highest duty.

Rabbinic teaching is too pervasively instinct with ethical motivations to permit this dangerous confusion of means and ends. There were times when historical circumstances compelled a psychological withdrawal into self and a consequent glorification of self on the part of Jews. The concept of the "Chosen People" underwent many fluctuations—the pendulum swung between a narrow exclusiveness and a broad comprehensiveness. But Jewish tradition always retained reminders and safeguards designed to prevent a temporary mood of self-exaltation and pride from becoming the abiding philosophy of the group. The Bible is by no means given over solely to the praise of Israel. Someone, with only apparent jocularity, once described the Bible as the world's most anti-Semitic book. No other national literature abounds in such extensive and pointed self-criticism. Time and again the people is rebuked and castigated. The words of the prophets are often like stinging whip lashes upon the body-politic of the group to which it is addressed, and no stronger indictment of Israel can probably be found anywhere than in the opening chapter of Isaiah—an indictment which to this day is publicly read in the Synagogue.

The Rabbis appropriated this tradition of self-criticism and incorporated it into their outlook. When Jerusalem was destroyed and its Temple burnt, the rabbis bade their people look inward, not outward. The mood they sought to stimulate was not self-pity but self-judgment and self-examination. It would have been easy to blame the invader and exculpate oneself. "Jerusalem was destroyed," the rabbis reminded their defeated community, "because dishonesty was rampant"; "because hatred of one's fellows was widespread"; "because judgment was rendered exclusively, according to the strict letter of the law"; "because the children were neglected." Above and beyond the people were God and His moral law. When a group sets itself up above the law and makes its own welfare and power the ultimate criterion of right, it courts disaster. In the arena of history, such rebelliousness does not go unpunished. No nation enjoys such a favored relationship with God as to be exempt from the inexorable working of the moral law. "And ye shall be holy men unto Me" (Exodus 22.30), declares the Bible. A sage succinctly comments, "If you are holy, then are you mine."

The concept of a universal God acted as a restraint upon the tendency of nationalism to become exclusive. Even the empires that were the historic foes of Israel in ancient times were not outside the purview of God's interest. Thus the Bible joins two of these empires to the name of Israel when affirming God's universal dominion: "In that day shall Israel be a third unto Egypt and Assyria, a blessing in the midst of the land. Whom the Lord of Hosts hath blessed saying, 'Blessed be Egypt My People and Assyria the work of My hands and Israel My Heritage.' " (Isaiah 19.24, 25). Israel was "chosen" not in violation of a moral law, which would disallow favoritism, but in order to advance and fulfill that law by its dedication and sacrifice. Its selection was not for domination but for service. The Rabbis interpreted the doctrine of a "Chosen People" as the assumption of greater responsibility. In divorcing it from any purpose of self-glory and aggrandizement, they did not find it incompatible with their concept of a God who rules over all mankind. That this idea has in it the seeds of chauvinism cannot be denied. Seen in the context of the total outlook of the Rabbis, it is an expression of the belief that Israel has an important role in the history of humanity. The fact that Israel was "chosen" did not mean that it could not be "rejected" when its conduct made it undeserving and unqualified to carry the great burden of responsibility that was imposed upon it.

V. *"The Powers that be Are Ordained of God"* (Romans 13.1 ff.). This Pauline idea, repeated many times in the New Testament (Titus 3.1; I Peter 2.13 ff.; Matthew 22.21) gives theological sanction to a doctrine which has worked much harm in human history, namely, "The king can do no wrong." This view is in direct contrast to both Biblical and Rabbinic teaching.

The fuller statement of the Apostle illumines his point of view. "Let every one be in subjection to the authorities that are set over him, for no authority exists unless by God's will, and those who actually exist have been appointed by him, so that one who arrays himself against the authority puts himself in opposition to the ordinance of God, and those who oppose this will bring judgment on themselves."

No reference needs to be made to the dramatic and courageous struggle which prophets waged against oppressive and unjust monarchs. Already in Deuteronomy do we find enunciated the principle that the king is not above the law, as opposed to the theory that the king is the source and author of all law. He, like all men, is subject to the law and "must not stray from the commandment, to the right or left" (Deuteronomy 17.15 ff.). The dangers of the usurpation of power by a ruler were never more clearly or more eloquently set forth than in the words spoken by the prophet to the elders who came to him to ask that a king be set over them (I Samuel, Chapter VIII). Above government, as above all history, was God. Saul, the first king of Israel, was deposed when he presumed to govern in violation of the law. The Bible condemns those kings of Judea and Israel whose rule was marked by evil and injustice. It is not stretching modern phraseology to describe the king under Jewish law as a "constitutional monarch." In the last analysis the people were to be ruled by "a government of laws" and not "a government of men." The successful revolt against Syrian oppression of the Jewish religion was followed by a renewal of Jewish monarchy. The political and religious policies of the Hasmonean kings and princes during the period of independence were such that the people turned against them in resentment and anger. Their place in history is not an honored one. "Do not stand in an evil thing" (Ecclesiastes 8.3) justifies disobedience to a king who commands his subjects to do evil. Judaism never accepted what Alexander Pope called, "the right divine of kings to govern wrong." "The rights of sovereignty" were always to be subject to the "sovereignty of rights." [*]

Nowhere in Jewish law or legend is there a reference to a divine ancestry of kings. When Roman emperors who regarded themselves as deities placed their image in the Temple at Jerusalem, the people rose in rebellion. Josephus has preserved a description of the touching scene when multitudes marched to the palace of the Procurator in Caesarea with their wives and children and uplifted their throats to the swords of the Roman legionnaires rather than return without a promise that the offensive statue would be removed. There were no images of the kings of Israel and not even the most beloved among them was believed to be more than mortal. In a universe governed by a moral God, the rule of no man was to be absolute.

The attitude of the Rabbis was not anarchic rejection of human authority. They knew the chaos and violence that fill the vacuum caused by the absence of proper authority. "Men would swallow one another alive," sadly reflects a Rabbi, "were it not for fear of the government."[7] Did not Jeremiah address these words to those who went forth into exile, "Seek the welfare of the city whither I have caused you to be carried away captive, and pray unto the Lord for it; for in its welfare shall ye have welfare"? (Jeremiah 29.7). In the third century C. E., the great Babylonian teacher, Mar Samuel, summarized the Jewish attitude in three Aramaic words which have become famous in Jewish tradition: "Dina d'malchuta dina" — "the law of the state is binding." Commentators and interpreters have carefully delimited the application of this principle. The law of the state is binding when it is established and enforced by duly constituted authority; when it embraces equally all classes of men and does not require its citizens to violate their religious conscience. Government is not only necessary because men are evil and should be restrained, but also because men are good and should be aided. There are many areas of service and welfare which no collective smaller than government could undertake. When government, however, invades the "inalienable rights" of its citizens, rights which it did not confer and which it has no authority to revoke, it is the duty of God-fearing and freedom-loving men to resist its encroachments.

XIII

THE ENDURING WORTH
OF THE TALMUD

Have we, in our consideration of the Talmud and its development, engaged in an excursion into history, in a conscious recall of an institution of the past? Have we simply made a pious pilgrimage to distant forebears, visiting the scenes of their labors, examining the fruit of their work? Has ours been a gesture of reverence, an exercise of curiosity, a flight from the immediate to the remote — and nothing more? Or has the subject of our study a significance that transcends its own period and flows over into our own day and needs? Is there contemporary value in our concern with this literature of the past? Does a voice speak out of the Talmud to men living centuries away and universes removed from the social and intellectual world in which they who fashioned it taught and reflected? What, if any, is the abiding and permanent significance of the Talmud for modern men who cannot accept in full the premises upon which the Rabbinic way of life rests and will not order their behavior to accord with the disciplines it ordains?

For the unquestioning believer in the tradition as it has come down, the boundaries between the past and the present literally disappear. He continues to live in the universe of ideas out of which the Talmud came and he recognizes no great gap between ancestry and posterity. He accepts the authority of the Talmud and lives by its prescriptions. Whatever changes the centuries have wrought have taken place within the prescribed framework of its system, utilizing the flexibility which its procedures permit. There has been no change in the strict traditionalist's attitude to the Talmud, nor any weakening of the place it holds as the arbiter of what is right in belief and practice. In the Yeshivot — the orthodox academies of higher learning — the Talmud is studied as a guide to present-day living; its ordinances enjoy today the same sanction and authority they did in the past.

Here we have one of the influences of the Talmud that has carried over into contemporary life. Though statistics are unavailable, it is safe to state that many Jews — perhaps several millions — throughout the world are governed to this day in their religious outlook by the Talmud. Whatever exercises as immediate and visible an impact upon the lives of so considerable a segment of Jewry obviously has interest for all who are concerned with life in our times generally and Jewish life in particular.

Moreover, until the very threshold of our era — and modern life for East European Jews who constitute by far the majority of the Jews of the world began in this century — the Talmud was guide and authority for the largest section of them. It is safe to say that the grandfather, and certainly the great-grandfather of the second or third generation native-born American Jew who may be reading these pages, has with few exceptions lived in accordance with the way of life charted by the Talmud. If this recent ancestor was a man who had received higher training in Jewish law and thought, his mental and spiritual outlook markedly bore the stamp of Talmudic influence. However, if circumstances had deprived him of the opportunity for any but an elementary education, the possibilities are great that he was reared in an environment in which many informal influences, traceable to the Talmud and its teachings, played upon him. The regimen of observances which he followed, the folklore which was recounted to him, phrases and idioms which spiced the Yiddish he spoke, stories and hero-figures which were told and spoken of in his hearing, represented a direct impinging upon him of the Talmud whose pages he never studied. However great the social transformations which have shaken our world during the past two or three generations, there still persists a line of continuity between grandfather and grandchild.

If the non-conforming Jew has not cast out every vestige of his ancestral tradition, but has affiliated with one of the more liberal branches of Judaism current in our communities, the impact of the Talmud will be visible, in however limited a degree, in his own life as well. If his wife lights candles on the eve of Sabbath or if they are kindled in the temple or synagogue of his choice; if his son becomes Bar Mitzvah; if benedictions are pronounced at his marriage service; if he holds a Jewish Prayer-book in his hand, however greatly it may differ from the traditional; if he cites the "Shema" as the great watchword of his faith; if a weekly portion of the Torah is read on the Sabbath; and if he refers to the spiritual leader of his Congregation as Rabbi, he is being guided by the men of the Talmud. Should he ever discourse on the basic ideas of Judaism, its social doctrines or the sensitivities it seeks to inspire — he could not escape including, though unawares, elements and emphases for which the tradition is indebted to Rabbinic Judaism. The Talmud therefore cannot be relegated to the past as long as it continues to direct thought and action on the part of living men.

The lasting importance of the Talmud, however, is not yet adequately described. Seen from the largest perspective, the Talmud represents one of the most impressive attempts in history to build what has been variously called "the good society," "the City of God," "the world perfected under the kingdom of God," "the ethical life." Neither unmindful of economic and social realities nor overwhelmed by them, disregarding neither the urgencies of the time in which they lived nor the frailties to which man is heir, — the Rabbis pursued with rare consistency the goal of a collective life governed by moral purposes and standards. They recognized that to attain this goal it is necessary both to educate and elevate the individuals who comprise the community, as well as to create the social conditions and establish the institutions supporting such an objective. They did not permit themselves to be impaled either on the horn of collectivism or that of individualism in the program they sought to implement. Theirs was what we would describe today as a God-centered outlook, though it is not possible to exaggerate the role which humane interests and motives occupied in their thought. Their vocabulary was essentially religious and their fundamental views were cast in a theological mold. Their purposes were, as has been indicated, social and practical, even as their criteria and principles were essentially ethical and moral. The ultimate sanctity of life, says the prophet, is to be found in righteousness and justice (see Isaiah 5.16). Utopias projected by the creative imagination of philosophers and novelists have claimed the attention of generations of students and readers who, recognizing the imperfections of their own societies, have sought inspiration and counsel for their improvement. In the Talmud, we have a legal and ethical system which, though not detached from an actual community, always held ideal ends before it.

If the Bible, as has often been pointed out, is revered but not read in Western civilization, the Talmud is neither regarded nor studied. Of all the great classics that the human spirit has produced, it is the least known by the world and exerts therefore the least influence upon the thought of educated men. The stimulation it might provide in the area of our major confusions and dilemmas is withheld because the Talmud remains a closed book. The ethical resources with which it is filled and the record of the great experiment to which allusion has been made, which it embodies, could throw significant rays of light upon the problems with which mankind is presently grappling. The wisdom of the Talmud suggests another of its enduring values.

The Talmud confronts us not only with its contents, but also with an important emphasis on method. We have seen that its ruling motivation was the achievement of an ethical life for the community and its individual citizens. The nature of this goal and the methods to be employed in reaching it are discussed in the Talmud in innumerable ways. Basically the approach of the Talmud is a rational one. To be sure the Rabbis were men of faith and were committed to convictions not completely amenable to rational proof. They were men of emotion whose loyalty to their tradition and attachment to their people were deep and moving. Citations in evidence of the intensity of their feelings could be easily multiplied. Yet it is equally true that they were men of reason. Their temper was intellectual, their method rational.

A thoughtful scholar pointed out in a recent book, about Judaism "It (Judaism) did not restrict itself to rationalism, but it never justified itself by anti-rationalism."[1] Religion that does not stand in awe before the profound mystery of the universe nor bow in reverence and humility before its Creator, nor respond with love to the Cosmic Father, nor react with a sense of unworthiness to the overwhelming consciousness of man's weakness and limitations — such a religion is bereft of the hallmarks of a great faith. But a religion that does not examine its premises, that is scornful of reason, that frees its yearnings and pieties from all rational discipline, that throws off all intellectual restraints, opposes investigation and analysis and prefers to be guided solely by its intuitions and mystic gropings is a religion susceptible to excess, prone to superstition and ever in peril of losing its soul as well as its mind. The rational order that does not know how to tap deep emotions in its behalf will not prevail over anti-rational doctrines that cleverly manipulate and mobilize the passions of people. Reason can save us from the tyrannies of passion and dogma. Emotion can provide the power to translate the cognitions of the mind and the insights of the spirit into the realities of our personal life and our social structure. We are here faced by no academic issue. If the minds of men are to be enlightened, their hearts too must be won. In the Talmud, were we to open our eyes to its instruction, we have an outstanding guide-book, so to speak, for the attainment of a proper balance.

We have noted that the forms of Jewish life in synagogue procedure and personal religious practice largely derive from the Talmud. While it may be a sign of sophistication to scoff at the ritual aspect of religion, the observances and symbols have historically played a great role in the survival of Judaism. As Milton Steinberg has put it, "the ideas and ideals of a people may give it significance but its group habits give it life." A people which was excluded from the society about it was enabled through its procedures and practices to fashion an environment of its own. Displaced, the Jew had what has been called a "compensating culture" of his own. The forms which Rabbinic law provided were not empty vessels. Into them had been poured a spirit which even routinization could not completely throttle. They inspired a sense of duty; they made for habits of moderation; they served as a link between an individual and a tradition; they reminded the Jew of his past and stirred within him hopes for promised redemption in the future; they brought the poetry of the rite and the symbol into lives that might otherwise have been unbearably prosaic; they united the far-flung communities in which a dispersed people lived; they fostered attitudes of mutuality and responsibility and helped a group retain a high degree of self-respect and dignity in circumstances which otherwise might well have crushed the last vestige of faith in self. The observances were outward manifestations of a historic identity and continuity. They were thus able to free the Jew from the tyranny of a dismal present and make him see himself from a larger and liberating perspective. But more than that. The observances were expressions of a duty that devolved upon him. He was set upon the stage of history to testify to the presence of God in human affairs and in the supremacy of His law over all man-made mandates. None of the social disabilities or physical degradations that were forced upon the Jew could expunge the cosmic significance which was his.

Whatever the Jew's social or physical fate was, he

himself never became uprooted. He bore, so to speak, his roots within himself. Fate recurringly compelled him to seek new habitations. These physical transplantations did not destroy the continuity he felt and maintained with his history and tradition. Whenever religious frenzy, political disturbance or economic crisis drove him into exile, he took with him a stabilizing regimen, an established way of life. Whenever ten Jews assembled, a community, ordered and rooted, came into being. The myth of the "Wandering Jew" could have been created only by those who, looking from the outside, saw merely the externalities of migration which were forced upon him. The history of the Jew as it appears from his own memoirs, chronicles a settled life, often in the midst of turbulence and insecurity, of communities governed by respected leaders, in accordance with accepted norms and procedures, in conformity with an established law.

NOTES

NOTES

II

ATTEMPTING A DEFINITION

1. *Studies in Judaism*, 3rd series.

III

THE RISE OF THE ORAL LAW

[1] *Vita Mosis* quoted in Moore's *Judaism* I, 269.
[2] Abot V, 25.
[3] G. F. Moore, *Judaism* II, 25.
[4] Rosh Hashana 25b.

IV

WHY ORAL?

[1] *Gaonic Responsa* ed. by B. M. Levin in footnote to Iggeret Sherira, 22.

V

THE MISHNA

[1] Canticles Rabba II. 5.
[2] Sifre, Deuteronomy.
[3] Gittin 4, 5.
[4] Baba Metzia 4, 10.
[5] Baba Metzia 7, 1.

VI

THE GEMARA

[1] Gittin 60b.

VII

HALACHA AND AGGADA

[1] L. Ginzberg, *Students, Scholars and Saints*, pp. 1, 2.
[2] G. F. Moore, *Judaism* I, 140.
[3] Abot, IV.
[4] Gustav Karpeles, *Jewish Literature and Other Essays*, p. 55 ff.

IX

THE RELIGION OF THE RABBIS

[1] G. F. Moore, *Judaism*, I. 361.
[2] A. H. Silver, *Where Judaism Differed*, p. 30.
[3] Tosefta, Shebu'ot III, 6.
[4] Exodus Rabba, Yithro XXIX, §5.
[5] Deuteronomy Rabba, II, §31.
[6] Megilla 13a.
[7] *Some Aspects of Rabbinic Theology*, pp. 36 ff.
[8] G. F. Moore, *Judaism*, I. 375.
[9] Genesis Rabba, *Lekh Lekha* XXXIX §6.
[10] G. F. Moore, *Judaism*, I. 479.
[11] Abot III, 19.
[12] Esther Rabba, 23, 1.
[13] Talm. Jerushalmi Succah, 4:3.
[14] G. F. Moore, *Judaism*, I. 229-30.

X

ASPECTS OF RABBINIC SOCIAL TEACHING

[1] Shabbat 82a.
[2] Leviticus Rabba 34, 9.
[3] Shabbat 63a.
[4] Berachot 17.
[5] Kiddushin 17.
[6] Baba Metzia, 109.
[7] Cf. S. Atlas, *Yearbook CCAR*, LIV, pp. 212-41.

XI

JUSTICE AND COURTS

[1] Abot I, 18.
[2] Pesikta d'Rabbi Kahana 140b.
[3] Shabbat 10a.
[4] Sifra 89a.
[5] Makkot 1, 10.

XII

THE DENIALS OF RABBINIC TEACHING

[1] Abot II, 6.
[2] Nedarim 41a.
[3] Baba Metzia 59b.
[4] Tanna d'bei Eliyahu p. 48.
[5] Lamentations Rabba 1, 33.
[6] Cf. Atlas, *op. cit.*
[7] Abot III, 2.

XIII

THE ENDURING WORTH OF THE TALMUD

[1] A. H. Silver, *op. cit.*, p. 2.

BIBLIOGRAPHY

BIBLIOGRAPHY

The following books will be helpful for further study. They have been selected both for their intrinsic value and ready availability to the English reader.

*　　*　　*

Soncino Press — *The Talmud* (In English) — *The Midrash* (In English)

Baeck, L. — *The Essence of Judaism*

Bamberger, Bernard — *The Story of Judaism* (Chapters 18–21)

Baron, Salo — *A Social and Religious History of the Jews*, Vol. II, pp. 215–321

Bokser, B. Z. — *The Wisdom of the Talmud*

Caplan and Ribalow (editors) — *Great Jewish Books*, pp. 59–91

Cohen, A. — *Everyman's Talmud*

Danby, H. — *The Mishna* (English translation)

Finkelstein, L. (editor) — *The Jews*, Vol. I, pp. 115–201
— *Akiba*

Ginzberg, Louis — *Students, Scholars and Saints*, pp. 35–124 — *Jewish Law and Lore*, pp. 3–57 — *The Legends of the Jews* (7 volumes)

Glatzer, N. — *Hillel the Elder: the Emergence of Classical Judaism*

Goldin, J. — *The Living Talmud*

GRAETZ, H. — *History of the Jews*, Vol. II, pp. 451–635

HERTZ, J. H. — *Ethics of the Fathers*

HERFORD, R. TRAVERS — *The Pharisees*

KADUSHIN, M. — *The Rabbinic Mind*
— *Organic Thinking in Rabbinic Thought*

KOHLER, K. — *Jewish Theology*

LAUTERBACH, J. Z. — *Rabbinic Essays*

LEARSI, R. — *Israel*, Chapters 24–28

MARGOLIS and MARX — *History of the Jews*, Chapters 34–37

MOORE, GEORGE FOOT — *Judaism* (3 volumes)

SCHECHTER, SOLOMON — *Studies in Judaism* — first series, pp. 182–212 — second series, pp. 102–125 — third series, pp. 194–237
— *Some Aspects of Rabbinic Theology*

SCHWARTZ, LEO (editor) — *Great Ages and Ideas of the Jewish People*

SILVER, ABBA HILLEL — *Where Judaism Differed*

STEINBERG, MILTON — *The Making of the Modern Jew*, pp. 47–62; 80–120
— *As a Driven Leaf* (novel)
— *Basic Judaism*

STRACK, H. — *Introduction to the Talmud and Midrash*

TRATTNER, E. — *Understanding the Talmud*

WAXMAN, MEYER — *A History of Jewish Literature*, Vol. I, Chapters 2, 5, 6

ZEITLIN, S. — *The Second Commonwealth*

DATE DUE

JUL 2 2 1993			